94 CREATIONS 6

Editor in Chief
Adriena Dame

Co-Managing Editors
Amy Jackson
Angela Jackson-Brown
Laura Caitlin Davis

Editors
Erin Pike
Charlene Luck
Carmen Brown
Patti Charron
Julia Crittendon
Elizabeth Filiatreau
Nuray Yasalanyar

94 Creations, founded in 2007 and relaunched in 2012, is a literary journal committed to celebrating previously unpublished fiction, creative nonfiction, drama, poetry, and whatnot. The editorial team exercises creative license to vary the overall presentation of this book from issue to issue, and is committed to publishing a collection of work at least once a year.

94 Creations
www.94creations.com

978-0-9857056-5-7

94CREATIONS6

PUBLISHER'S NOTE

94 Creations is a print literary journal committed to publishing an eclectic assortment of outstanding fiction, creative nonfiction, poetry, drama, and art by both emerging and established writers and artists. We welcome the gritty, offbeat, marvelous works often overlooked in mainstream publishing venues, as well as those works that create an authentic experience within the framework of more conventional literary landscapes. We are also interested in celebrating diversity, and are eager to attract the attention of exceptional writers of beautifully varied backgrounds.

Narvelle Jasmine Alexander Littleton (1913-2007), my grandmother, was a significant inspiring force behind the founding of this publication. Despite the hardships of raising nine children in rural Arkansas during a time when racism and sexism prevailed, she found countless ways to exercise her creativity, and to thrive as an artist. I am proud to be a part of the legacy she helped to forge.

I am also thankful for the phenomenal editors, whose love, respect, friendship, time, energy, and teamwork have made this issue possible. Effusive thanks to Amy, for effectively managing our editorial ebb and flow; to Angela, for her meticulous and timely attention to detail, and for accepting the invitation to join Amy as co-managing editor; to Erin, Julia, Nuray, and Char, for reading, reading, reading submissions and proofreading copy; and to our new editors, Patti and Carmen, for fitting right in as if they have been in the mix from the start.

I believe that *every* submission is valuable, tangible, inspiring evidence that writers are out there, daring to share their creations at the risk of rejection, and at the risk of acceptance. Thus, my gratitude for all of the artists whose creative works appear herein, and all of the artists who sought, but did not achieve, publication with us this time around, is boundless.

Thank you for your interest in *94 Creations*. We look forward to your readership for many issues to come.

~ Adriena Dame

EDITORIAL TEAM

Adriena Dame, author of *The Moo: Stories and a Novella* and publisher of *Iris Brown Lit Mag*, teaches undergraduate creative writing and literature courses at Spalding University. She conducts them-based writing workshops for public school teachers and community-based organizations, teaches English as a Second Language to adult learners, serves as a board member for Louisville Literary Arts, and is a youth writing coach for Generation iSpeak. As co-owner of SOSAJI! & Co., a Louisville, Kentucky boutique on a mission to build a legacy of giving, gumption, and goodwill, Adriena designs SOSAJI! socks, creates hand-made jewelry art, and works at promoting other artists.

Amy Jackson is a fiction writer who grew up in southeastern Kentucky and wandered around Providence, Rhode Island and San Francisco before finally heeding the call to come back to the South. She has an MA in English from the University of Kentucky and wrote her thesis on Lewis Carroll and the relationship between writer and reader. Amy currently lives in Louisville, Kentucky with her dog Lucky and is working on her first novel.

Angela Jackson-Brown is the author of *Drinking From a Bitter Cup*, published in 2014 by WiDo Publishing, is a poet and writer residing in Indianapolis, Indiana. She is an English professor at Ball State University and a graduate of the Spalding University's low-residency MFA in Writing Program. Her work appears in *Pet Milk*, *The Louisville*

Review, *New Southerner Literary Magazine*, *94 Creations* and *Muscadine Lines: A Southern Journal*. Her short story, "Something in the Wash," was awarded the 2009 fiction prize by *New Southerner Literary Magazine* and was nominated for a Pushcart Prize in Fiction.

Laura Caitlin Davis is a student in Spalding University's low-residency MFA in Writing Program, and holds a BA in Anthropology from the University of Louisville. She has worked as an editor for several years. Her stories appear in The Heartland Review and The One Million Stories Project. On her wrist, she sports a black and purple tattoo she calls her "perpetual purple prompt." It reads Ecrivez, a French word that essentially means, "Dude, you better write!"

Erin Pike is an attorney by day and a fiction writer by night. Born and raised in Louisville, Kentucky, Erin attended the University of Louisville, where she received a BA in Philosophy and graduated with honors. She went on to receive her JD from the University of Louisville Brandeis School of Law, after which she spent several years writing and researching for judges in her state's highest courts. Erin now spends her free time writing novel-length fiction for young adults. She is currently a student in the MFA in Writing For Children and Young Adults program at Vermont College of Fine Arts.

Charlene Luck is a fiction writer from the Greater Detroit Area. She is a graduate of the University of Michigan's MFA in prose program, where she completed her thesis, a collection of short stories titled "In Your Houses." Her short story, "Grey Herons," was a finalist in the Glimmer Train Stories Summer Short-Short Fiction Contest 2007. She lives in Louisville, Kentucky with her husband, Jeff, and three cats: Manny, Mike, and Cheszwyck.

Carmen Brown is a Kentucky-born AfroLatina hellbent on changing the world one word at a time.

Patti Charron is a writer and editor based in Louisville, Kentucky. Dangling modifiers get on her nerves.

Elizabeth Filiatreau has had a hand in grant writing, newspaper editing, and publishing as a guest columnist in the Courier-Journal. After years of following other people's dreams, she is in pursuit of her own brand of happiness, which includes becoming a successful writer. She has two children and two grandchildren, and she lives in Louisville, Kentucky with her dogs, Mabel and Zoey Doodle, who only interrupt her writing when it interferes with their suppertime.

Julia Crittendon is the publisher of *Metamorphosis: Inspirational Stories of Women Living with Alopecia* (her success story is featured in the December/January 2012 issue of *Ebony Magazine*). A woman of many hats, she is co-founder of SOSAJI! & Co. boutique and SOSAJI! brand products; she works as a personal trainer, fitness coach, and phlebotomist; and she is the director of Generation iSpeak, a youth-centered non-profit organization designed to facilitate learning and exploration in the areas of literacy, arts, and education.

Nuray Yaşayanlar is from the old stomping ground of Homer, Izmir, Tŭrkiye and lives in Louisville, Kentucky. She graduated from Hacettepe University's English Language and Literature Department and earned an MA in Teaching from Spalding University. While she most enjoys writing poetry and creative nonfiction, her writing life began with journalistic flair during her high school years; she would pen editorials in her blue, leather-covered journals after watching the evening news. Her fellowship with Louisville Writing Project fired her creative passion, and her participation in Mixed Nuts Writers Group continues to fuel her commitment to writing. Currently, she teaches English at Central High School.

CONTENTS

MARIANNE WORTHINGTON is co-founder and poetry editor of *Still: The Journal*, an online literary magazine. She also serves as poetry editor for *Now & Then: The Appalachian Magazine*. She edited the first three volumes in the *Motif* anthology series for MotesBooks. She lives, writes and teaches in southeastern Kentucky.

ON SEEING A LETTER PATSY CLINE WROTE TO NUDIE THE TAILOR, RECEIVED MARCH 6, 1963

Her handwriting sways like a song

Dear Mr. Nuddie, I have put on paper
a picture of two dresses I'd like you
to make for me if you can and hope
you can understand how I want them made.

in dull pencil on dime-store tablet paper.
The rodeo tailor's name is misspelled
but other details are exact:

My measurements are to the very inch:
Bust 34 D, Waist 25 inches, Hips 38 inches.

A real woman's shape will swing
toward the microphone, ache
and yearning will glitter her voice,

I would like the one dress in white
with rhinestones and the shirt in a sky blue
and rhinestones on the cuffs,

I would also like a silver cape made to throw
around my shoulders.
I've made a drawing of that too.

I don't want leather in the cape. I'd rather have
a silver material, lined with red satin inside.

And how long will it take you to make them?

and a flash will come.

She will remember the red cowgirl suit
sewn by her mother, wagon wheels
and rhinestones burden the hem.

Just a day after the wreckage still
smoldered nose-first in the murky woods,
the letter arrived in California.

Forever we search for the spangle and sequin.
Forever we follow her calligraphed tones.

A.P. CARTER V. SARA CARTER, 1932

after Tyehimba Jess

Her voice was deep as Copper Creek—
rough as the white oak on Clinch Mountain;
she was singing something lonesome,
leaves sifting the sound,
floated down like I
had to find it and my mission: to doctor songs;
and follow a black man through
all the places I couldn't go, closed up to me
wary, guarded—I walked the tracks toward
a life of music and Sara, prettier than
the songs. Again, I left my mother,

Heard me singing "Lonesome Valley"
name like the place where we lived;
heard me singing while he was selling fruit trees
swaying me to think it was me he
wanted, but it wasn't. No,
he wanted me and Maybelle to traipse
all over creation dragging our babies around
like guitar cases. Finally I said
the plain truth: I love Coy Bayes better than
anything I ever laid eyes on. I left
the songs, left my children.

Goodbye Poor Valley

I couldn't stop searching for that sound.

I never could make anybody understand.

STEVE KLEPETAR teaches literature and writing at Saint Cloud State University in Minnesota. His work has received several nominations for the Pushcart Prize and Best of the Net. His latest collections include *Speaking to the Field Mice* (Sweatshoppe Publications), *Blue Season* (with Joseph Lisowski, mgv2>publishing), and *My Son Writes a Report on the Warsaw Ghetto* (Flutter Press). An e-chapbook, *Return of the Bride of Frankenstein*, is forthcoming from Kind of a Hurricane Press.

ALL OF MY HUNGERS

All of my hungers sing
in this space between my ears
my mouth with its lolling tongue
taste buds ripening on the vine
of my flesh
my nose breathing in the muddy
scents of spring – leaves and worms
and rain
my eyes gobbling the gray sky
my wet skin reveling
in this new heaven of tingling cold

WHEN THE PARTY ENDED

When the party ended you folded
the room, that little cube
of space
you with your laughing
mouth, your crinkly cowgirl
eyes, and all of us
desperate in the wind.

All of us with our brooms
and dishcloths
fluttering in a staircase full of eyes.
When the party ended you carried
us off. We tumbled
in your purse
with keys, clatter of your change
leather in our nostrils, mint
and lilac and our frozen hands.

It seemed as if you stepped off the edge
of earth
as if all the maps were wrong
as if molecules had gone mad
wringing rain from all those boiling clouds.

PAUL ALBANO is a PhD candidate in fiction writing at the University of Louisiana at Lafayette. His work has appeared in *Cream City Review*, *MondayNight Lit*, and *Whiskey Island*, among other places.

THE BANKER

I

It is a warm summer evening and here at the end I am a sick man. At night I lie in bed, sleepless but inert, staring at the ceiling and the deep amber shaded knot that swirls above me like a tempest disturbing the placid surface of a cold and distant and oak-paneled ether. The doctors say I suffer from acute consumption and acute malaria and acute dengue fever and acute colon polyps and acute syphilis and acute diphtheria and just regular scurvy and a seeping gum infection they're not quite sure what to call but it seems acute along with poison ivy and old age and a psychosomatic case of trench foot, born from emotional distress and chronic melancholy and what appears to be a profound though otherwise latent desire to have trench foot. I tell the doctors they're fools, the whole rotten, foolish lot of them. Fools with blood-letting knives and tourniquet clothes bulging inside their breast pockets and belief in preposterous things like invisible pathogens and the convalescent value of a regulated diet. Let my diseases, all of them, including the imagined case of trench foot that I apparently also actually have, get worse I say. For unlike the crude beasts that stride through the hospital corridors with their limp-free gait and straight teeth and symmetrical faces, at least I am an attractive man. I can take solace in this. My hair grays fashionably at the temples, my eyes burn green, glowing like the foliage of an enchanted forest after weeks of rain, and my left cheek is bespeckled with a small vanity mole lying in the basin of my prominent zygomatic bone, while the right side of my face bears a decision I made late in life, my last great decision—to commission an elegantly rendered tattoo of a bird dry-humping a rhino etched across my cheek. It symbolizes something, the bird and the rhino and the dry-humping. I forget what.

II

But let me start at the beginning, for I was not always an old man. At age zero I was born. At age five I commenced a daily stretching exercise that I hoped would lead me to become an acrobat or at least flexible enough to stuff myself in drawers so as to startle whoever happened to open those drawers. At age ten I excelled at arithmetic and learned that if you divide any number in all the world, positive or negative, by that exact same number, this will yield the number one. Every time, without exception or variation because unlike the fickle world and the fickle people who populate it, arithmetic is not fickle. It is constant and unvarying, a truth in a universe of mendacity. Unless that number you're dividing is zero in which case no one is quite sure what to do. At age fifteen I grew an uneven mustache and realized for the first time that my father doesn't understand me and governs with a rather arbitrary and capriciously drawn set of rules which he himself often fails to uphold. At age twenty I became a banker and courted a woman with one eyebrow. At age twenty-five I married the woman with one eyebrow after notarizing a written promise from her to parse the one eyebrow into two eyebrows on or before the first year of our marriage. At age thirty I realized to my horror that no matter how many times my wife severs her one eyebrow the hair above the bridge of her nose will return, and once again the two eyebrows will unite and form one single monstrous eyebrow. At thirty-five I packed a trunk with clothes and money and left my wife, unable to bear the thought that one eyebrows are hereditary and would pass to any children we should have.

III

Years earlier, before now, I once received a telegram from Max Planck. It is my most prized possession. What I treasure above all other things. It read: *Dear The Banker STOP After years of math and thinking about math I have discovered that the laws governing the universe do not govern all parts of the universe and that there exist impossibly small and indivisible units of energy that operate under a wholly different and heretofore unknown set of physical laws STOP This has resulted in every belief and assumption I have ever held being torn asunder and also my eyesight diminishing STOP So now I wear glasses STOP With lenses like the bottom of mason jars STOP They do not look good STOP The glasses STOP In addition to the glasses the discovery has produced in me a deep feeling of what I will call regret STOP Each night I wander the cold and desolate streets of some lost town STOP Hungry and alone and ridden with despair STOP Haunted by the flickering memories of the truths I once believed in STOP Humanity means nothing to me STOP I cannot love cannot be infatuated cannot develop platonic friendships with attractive women that will one day lead to us having sex with each other after they discover that I know how to play the guitar STOP But will not lead to a committed relationship that would prohibit me from having sex with other women after they learn that I can play the guitar STOP I have learned to play the guitar for nothing STOP But possessing all of the world's knowledge has proven to have one benefit STOP I can see the future STOP I can gaze into the lusty mascaraed eyes of the new century that rapidly approaches at the same speed that every fixed date approaches but feels faster because of the significance of it and all that STOP And I have seen that the future will be unlike anything we can imagine STOP Wondrous in ways we cannot conceive STOP For in the future man will invent frying pans that food does not stick to STOP They will be called non-stick frying pans STOP And they will change everything*

IV

The second half of my life proceeded thusly: At age forty I moved to Moscow and learned that it was the capital of Russia and not Russia City which I had always thought. At age forty-five I bought a bank, in effect buying money with money, which forced me to acknowledge that I really don't know how banking works. At age fifty I read Anton Chekov's "The Bet," which inspired me to also bet some lawyer two million dollars that he couldn't live in a room in my house for fifteen years without any human contact, which he accepted, having not yet read the story himself. At age fifty-five I lost my fortune through bad luck and bad investments and compulsive additions to the black marble mausoleum I built so it would remain unfinished and I could therefore ward off death. At age sixty I saw a motion picture titled *The Great Train Robbery* and I was appalled. I stormed up to the projectionist's room and berated him for irresponsibly showing such drivel that not only glorifies unpardonable things like robbery and slowing trains down, but has the audacity to call such things great; which is a stance I clung to with fervency until the projectionist explained that "great" is not meant in the evaluative sense, but instead to denote something that's unusually or comparatively large in size or dimension, which is to say that robbing the train, while a morally repugnant act, was nevertheless a large scale undertaking that took planning and daring to execute and I said okay the title makes sense now. At sixty-five I plotted to kill the lawyer living in confinement in one of my spare rooms but didn't after I learned he had no designs on collecting the two million dollars I would've owed him but still I felt bad and like I kind of overreacted. At age seventy I began moving gingerly and remembering with immense fondness any moment from my past when I did not need to move so gingerly. At seventy-five I learned of opium and its applications and the ornately carpeted public houses in which it was frequently used. At age eighty the last strand of my hair finally abandoned me, like the coward I always knew it to be, and I was forced to spend the strained elasticity of my final days trying to convince others that I looked futuristic and not merely bald.

V

It was a winter evening, during one of those grand, operatic blizzards that's a part of our national character, unique only to Russia, and maybe the far reaches of

Greenland, and probably the northern masses of Canada and the eastern most points of Germany, likely all of Iceland and Estonia, and of course Finland and Norway and Sweden and any other country in Scandinavia that I may have omitted, and surprisingly enough Mongolia, that I fell in love. Her name was Svetlana. She was a woman. We met in a public coffee house. Her face looked good in the dim lighting but it was the kind of face that also would probably have looked good in bright light. We exchanged pleasantries at first, politely inquiring about each other's family history—I learned that her father owned a textile factory outside Saint Petersburg and anxiously awaited the prosperity the new century would bring—and then spent most of the next few hours discussing literature and politics and other things, like how there exists a country called England where everyone has names like Bob Cratchit and Tiny Tim and Ebenezer Scrooge and Ghost of Christmas Past, and how the world is twining into something so unrecognizable that you can now go into a hardware store and purchase a ladder built of aluminum instead of wood, and how sometimes you can talk to another person and know that you're both in agreement about some inviable but fundamental truth even without the other person nodding frequently at the things you say though that helps. And all while snowflakes like distant stars fell balletically from the night sky, which somehow seemed closer and less illusory than it ever had before. And then we parted ways, for this chance encounter occurred during one of the few intervals in which my wife did not have eyebrow hair growing above the bridge of her nose, and there was no way I could've known then that that wouldn't last.

MATTHEW BYRNE's poem "Let Me Count the Ways" was featured in *The Best American Poetry 2007*. He has been nominated twice for a Pushcart Prize, and received an International Merit Award from Atlanta Review in 2009. His chapbook, *Silent Partner*, won the 2013 Sow's Ear Press Chapbook Award. He received an MFA in poetry from the University of Montana in 1999, and now serves as vice president at an insurance agency in Chicago.

BUMPER STICKER

I was destined to adhere to your rear.
The end is near. I am an election won
that won't go away, a failed candidacy
preserved in sour grapes, a don't-blame-
me who told the goddamn tailgating so.
I am you boiled into a fine reduction.
Your conviction in suspended animation.
A comic strip character pissing impishly
upon the heraldry of your adversaries.
Our love is as undebatable as my message.
You picked me among the clamoring mob
at the interstate truck stop's gift shop.
I felt your pain. I promise to rein you in
if your perception starts to change.
I won't let you forget where you came from.

GRETCHEN CLARK has published work in *Hamilton Stone Review*, *Literary Mama*, *Word Riot*, *New York Family Magazine*, *Switchback*, and *Tiny Lights*, among others. She holds a B.A. in English and teaches creative nonfiction at Writers.com.

PINK CHRYSANTHEMUM

Love is reactive, not proactive, it arches backward.

~Lauren Slater, "True Love," *National Geographic*,
February 2006

1.

In spring 2012, on the first anniversary of our mother's death, my sister Joanne sent identical boxes to me and our two other sisters. Each box was decorated, shaped like a book with pink chrysanthemums adorning the cover. Inside were copies of our mother's recipes, a small vial of Kate Spade's Twirl perfume (a nod to her love of dance), a zip drive full of images, a photo album, and a purse-sized packet of Kleenex.

I sat the box on my desk and placed two photos atop it, one black and white, the other color. The first was a shot taken of my mother in her childhood backyard. She was eighteen, wearing a swimsuit and high heels, leaning against a lounge chair. The other picture showed my mother standing in the ocean, waves rolling across her model-long legs. She was only in her mid-twenties, but already mother to three little girls. She's wearing her signature red Janzen suit.

In both photos, my mother's face is half in shadow.

2.

After my mother died, I volunteered to write her eulogy. I wrote about her as a mother: the invaluable lessons about life and love she taught her four daughters. But I also talked about the moments when someone else peeked through, a woman unlike our attentive, saddle-oxford wearing mother. I wrote about a different kind of woman, one who performed a perfect cartwheel on the beach, often in her stunning, red Janzen swimsuit. A woman who ordered a Pink Lady cocktail – or three – during an occasional dinner out with her family, turning rosy-cheeked and giggly. A woman who signed up for belly dancing lessons at age fifty, the metal slap of her finger clackers sounding through our home while she practiced.

As I looked at the box and the photos, I found myself focusing on those flowers on the lid. In some countries, chrysanthemums symbolize death. In others, they stand for cheerfulness or honesty. I want to be honest about my mother.

My mother was a homemaker who gave me undivided attention. She sewed all my Halloween costumes, creating clothes for any character I wished to be. She made sure my black patent Mary Janes shone, my floral dresses were pressed, and my ponytails were perfect. She baked whatever I desired—banana bread, oatmeal cookies, mocha dream cake. She shuttled me to tap, jazz, ballet, and Polynesian dance classes. She took me to baton training, art lessons, and swim practice.

She made me feel special. That is part of the truth.

I saw my mother a week before she died. My sisters had stepped out of the hospital room for a moment. The effects of morphine and an emergency tracheotomy had left her unable to speak, but her eyes were open, looking at me. I took her hand, "I know we didn't always get along," I said, "but I want you to know that you were a good mother. I love you." It was true.

But what is the whole truth?

3.

Newly pregnant with me, my mother initially mistook her early symptoms for peri-menopause. At thirty-nine, she was already the mother of three teenage daughters. I was a surprise and shock; a pink caboose that screamed and cried with soul-crushing colic from dinner until early morning. I was the only one of her daughters afflicted with this mysterious, unabated crying that lasted for months.

4.

Theories about the root cause of colic abound: lactose intolerance, allergy, neurologic sensitivity. One study considered the relationship between maternal depressive symptoms and infant crying. It found that depressed mothers were more likely to have newborns who cried more.

5.

I remember an apartment we lived in briefly, when I was a six. My bedroom was on the second floor and faced the street below. Outside the window I could see the neatly clipped emerald field of my elementary school, ivy crawling up a nearby wooden fence, pines in the distance and a crimson ribbon of curb painted the same shade of red as my mother's Revlon lipstick.

My window on this world was draped in sheer yellow curtains. My dad would pull them back on Saturday mornings singing, "Rise and shine, sunshine." If that didn't rouse me he'd tickle the bottom of my soles through my thin Mickey Mouse sheets until I came to life.

Sometimes, on those Saturdays, my mom would run errands. I'd stay home with my dad, content to play dress-up with the family dog, Max, or to act out domestic bliss with Ken and Barbie in my vinyl and cardboard dollhouse. But if my mother hadn't returned by a certain point, I'd undress Max, leave the dolls sitting at their plastic kitchen table and go upstairs to my room to wait for her.

Pushing the happy-colored curtains aside, I'd open my bedroom window and perch on the cedar chest-turned-bench below. There, I'd watch and listen for my mother, using one finger to trace the length of the red emergency zone curb.

As I sat there, I'd imagine what might be keeping my mother. As the minutes ticked off, the images in my head grew more vivid and disturbing. I pictured my mother dead or dying in various dark poses; wearing a necklace of shattered windshield, a pink foam spilling from her now-colorless lips.

How could I get to her, I'd ask myself, growing more anxious. How could I help?

6.

As a child, I had frequent stomach aches. In kindergarten I had near-daily crying jags, episodes that were more than normal separation anxiety, and which lasted well into winter and beyond. Without provocation, I'd cry in the classroom or on the playground. When my exasperated teacher asked, "Why are you crying?" I was never able to articulate the deep sadness I felt. On the days I cried, my teacher pinned a note to my chest before I left school in the afternoon, addressed to my mother. "Gretchen was crying again…"

In addition to the tears, I had bouts of extreme rage that I directed toward myself. I'd pull out clumps of my hair and claw my skin, sometimes drawing blood. I bit myself, wanting to break the skin. I screamed and thrashed on my bedroom floor, pounding my fists, kicking my legs.

Because I never talked in class, my third-grade teacher suspected I might be suffering from a speech impediment and recommended I receive therapy. Twice a week, I was pulled out of class and sent to the speech therapist's room. There, I read aloud *From the Mixed-Up Files of Mrs. Basil E. Frankweiler,* then recited a poem the therapist had asked me to memorize. Afterward, I got to pick a prize from a shoebox – a beaded purse, a grape-scented eraser. I didn't go to these sessions for long, because the speech therapist could find nothing wrong.

My speech was normal, but looking back, I realize that something was clearly wrong. Type the symptoms of child anxiety into an Internet search, and many of my issues make the list. Something was eating at me, manifesting in physical symptoms and abnormal emotional outbursts.

7.

Chrysanthemums, commonly known as mums, are toxic.

8.

The color of the chrysanthemums petals on the box remind me of strawberry milk, a drink I enjoyed as a child. I remembered one morning, when I didn't have time to finish it, my mother covered the top of my glass with plastic wrap and put it in the refrigerator for later. After school, I reached for the glass, but condensation made it slip through my hand, and it crashed to the kitchen floor. Beneath my feet bloomed milk and glass.

The shattering glass cut through something unseen, and my mother's mood shifted. The shadow across her face appeared. She was upset, I knew, but she'd never say it. Even as I said, "Sorry," over and over, she ignored me, yanking me out of the way to grab a broom and dustpan, the scrape of my mistake crunchy and sharp in my ears. There was the shove of the garbage can, the slam of cupboards, the bang of the broom handle against the wall, often at the smallest provocation, even, yes, spilled milk. This was my mother's Morse code, and I became proficient in deciphering its unspoken messages. I was often on edge, waiting for this different mother to appear. This part of my mother turned my stomach acidic, triggered by body to pump the adrenaline of "fight or flight."

9.

A large number of aerophobic sufferers state trust as a contributing factor to their fear. They do not know the pilot, airline staff or security staff, or fellow passengers, and are very hesitant about trusting them to ensure a safe flight. This is especially poignant if the person has had problems with trusting relationships in the past, particularly as a small child.

~Jo Johnson, "Psychological Causes of Aerophobia." *Fear Free Flying,* September 2012

10.

Three years before our mother died my sister Joanne and I sat in the airport bar in Phoenix, waiting to board our flight to Rome. I washed down two anti-anxiety pills with a Long Island Iced tea. After takeoff, I ordered a Heineken and took another pill. I didn't fall asleep but somewhere over the Atlantic I was finally able to close my eyes.

On our fourth day in Rome, Joanne and I were on the escalator going up to the Vatican Museum when she elbowed me in the side. I turned to see my sister pointing at the backside of a woman standing in front of us. Sewn in black thread on her left jean pocket was Lois, our mother's name. My sister took a picture.

Later, Joanne sent me a file of her Italy shots. Under the photo she took of the woman on the escalator she added a caption: Mom genes.

Written in my sister's hand on the back of a different picture: Englewood Park 10/25/70.
I was age one. The loaf of bread at my sneakered feet suggested we were there to feed the ducks by the lake. My mother knelt behind me, her arms wrapped protectively around my body, keeping me safe. We're in matching coats of blue.

11.

Pregnant women with depression can pass the condition to their unborn babies, research has found.

~Daily Mail Reporter, "Babies can 'contract' depression in the womb: Infants with depressed mothers have abnormal brain wiring." *Daily Mail*, December 5, 2013

12.

I trace the pink flower petals with my finger. It's believed that the Chinese philosopher, Confucius, suggested chrysanthemums be used as objects of reflection.

I have two daughters, ages eighteen and twelve. When they were born, I willingly put any sort of career on the backburner. I've driven them to school, dance, track practice, gymnastics, art and music lessons. I've made their favorite meals, read them stories, cleaned up their messes, soothed their hurts and listened to them relay the ecstasy and anguish of their young lives. On a recent trip by myself to California my eighteen-year-old texted, "You haven't even been gone for eight hours and I already miss you!"

An unprompted note of affection from a teenage daughter is to be cherished. But I also know better. I know I can't point to this example and believe this proves I am a stellar mother, that my mothering record is unblemished. I know I have sometimes fallen short in ways I could easily tick off and in other ways I don't even realize. Only after years of doing the physical, psychological, emotional—and often exhausting—work of mothering have I come to understand that it is simply impossible for a child to reach adulthood without at least a couple black spots tucked into their memory when their mother fell short in some way. I know my daughters have their own strawberry milk stories to share, perhaps moments that will permanently affect them, that they may even have to work through.

13.

Three months after my first daughter was born I made an appointment to see a psychologist. Every Tuesday afternoon, as minutes ticked off on an egg timer, I cracked open. I shared the language of depression and silent rage I learned from my mother. The unsaid, that said so much.

14.

In May 2009 love arched me back home.

My mother had suffered grave complications from brain surgery to remove a benign tumor. Relocated from the hospital to a skilled nursing facility, a steady IV of morphine kept her quiet, still and rarely lucid. I sat at my mother's side, watching as my sister Joanne placed roses from our mother's garden beneath her nose so she could breathe in sweetness. A few darks specks of dirt clung to the stems.

An anagram of my mother's name is soil. In the rich, tenebrous mixture of my mother's love and mercurial moods I grew wild and quiet, deeply thoughtful, a little bit bitter, sharp-eyed and sharper-tongued. The years of rain, the little girl tears I shed, also made something unexpected flourish: empathy.

15.

In Europe, chrysanthemums are given as tokens of sympathy. I run my hands over the pink flowers and think of what my mother taught me. The importance of saying thank you, of being on time, of keeping my word. How to grow an avocado in a mason jar, how to get rid of hiccups (tablespoon of sugar), and how to pump my legs on a swing to go higher than the other kids.

But the most valuable lesson was only understood after she was gone: Not to see the world—or her—in black-and-white.

Sources

Slater, Lauren. "True Love." *National Geographic*, Feb. 2006. Web. 14 November 2013.

Johnson, Jo. "Psychological Causes of Aerophobia." *Fear Free Flying*, 30 Sept. 2012. Web. 3 January 2014.

Daily Mail Reporter. "Babies can 'contract' depression in the womb: Infants with depressed mothers have abnormal brain wiring." *Daily Mail*, 5 December 2013, Web. 24 April 2014.

TYLER KLINE balances his time between working on an organic vegetable farm and studying English at The University of Delaware. His work has appeared or is forthcoming in *East Coast Literary Review*, *Y'all'd've*, *Diverse Voices Quarterly*, and *The Camel Saloon*.

WHAT IF

Accustomed to larks humming
in the crowns of sycamores
and bees performing the tarantella:
over, under, and through thickets –
bidding summer a farewell with each buzz –
I was not ready for what I heard.
The woman telling her friend at her side
that her mother, *her mother*,

helped locate body parts, gray and mangled,
in that pile of building: nine-twelve-oh-one.

And as if emotions dined with thoughts
over wine the color of velvet
and a jazz record – agreeing
to trade places for a day –

I first *thought* of my mother and second
felt for my mother.
Circling around the budding thought: *what if?*
Feeling though, and desperately hoping,
please, not ever, *what if.*

RYAN TIPPETS is a photojournalist in the military. He has been published in *Heater*, *Shotgun Honey* and *The Molotov Cocktail*. He lives in New Orleans with his wife and three sons.

BIG HANDS, I KNOW YOU'RE THE ONE

When I was ten years old my one and only friend was Jeremy.

He was chubby enough to be called fat and had long, horse-like hair he kept in a ponytail that reached down to his waist. He wore these black shirts with wolves and dream catchers stretched across the chest. This was back before modern irony sucked the fun out of everything. He wore them because they were cool.

Massive coke bottle glasses dominated the top half of his face in a last ditch effort to provide him some kind of sight. He was legally blind. His eyes had the appearance of being untethered; they shook from side to side and vibrated up and down. And to top it all off, he smelled like an ashtray. To this day, I associate that smell with being poor.

Despite all the physical, economic, ocular and olfactory cards he had stacked against him, he was the coolest person I'd ever met.

He had an encyclopedic knowledge of all things awesome. He could list from memory every active wrestler in the WWF and the WCW. He could do the Wookie voice like you wouldn't believe. He had a love for Batman most parents reserve for their first-born child.

And he could play the kazoo like a motherfucker.

I was Robin to his Batman, he was Short Round to my Indy, he was Chewbacca to my Han, or vice versa. We traded that one off. Not Luke though. We were never Luke. We both agreed Luke was a pussy.

He was my road dog.

The day the Earth's poles reversed was my mom's turn to drop me off at Jeremy's trailer. We pulled down his gravel road and ended up at an empty driveway. I heard my mom suck her teeth and say, "Shirlene," and then she shook her head. Jeremy's mom was always leaving him stranded all alone against the natives. Not that he ever complained. "Better a king in a lonely castle than not being a king at all." He said funny things like that.

When we climbed out of our minivan Wayne and Grayson came running towards us at a dead sprint. His dogs loved me, but they loved jumping on my mom even more.

Answering my mom's shouts, Jeremy opened the screen door to his trailer and stepped down.

"Wayne, Grayson, get down off of Miss Loraine. Get."

The dogs lowered themselves but circled us and wagged their tails.

Instead of high-fiving me like a normal kid would, Jeremy crouched down and did his best impersonation of a movie announcer's voice: "If adventure has a name, it must surely be…Toby Williams!"

We busted up laughing. Inserting ourselves into movie taglines was one of our specialties.

He walked over and offered his hand to my mom.

"How are you Miss Loraine? Thank you so much for bringing Toby out."

"Oh, no problem Sweetie. Toby's been begging me all day to bring him out here. Say, is your mom out at the store?"

I could tell by the way Jeremy blushed that he rather wouldn't say where his mom was. My mom could, too.

"Oh, never mind. Just have her call me when you see her, ok? You boys have fun now, and don't go near that trestle. I mean it."

We both lied to my mother's face. She kissed my forehead and said goodbye to Jeremy and drove off down the road.

We looked at each other, bowed, and took off running and hollering through the pasture behind Jeremy's trailer.

Three hundred yards behind his trailer is the Chief Ladiga Trail. It's over thirty miles of paved bike path that travels through forest and pasture. It combines with the Silver Comet Trail and eventually ends up in Georgia. For two unsupervised adventurers, it was Dagobah. It was the Thunderdome. It was the Temple of Doom.

It was ours.

The Alabama summer heat launched a full frontal assault on our tiny bodies, but it was no match for the ferocity of youth.

Approaching the trail, we picked out a couple of sticks appropriately sized to suit our needs. Jeremy stepped onto the trail first, turned, and held his sword out to the side.

"I knew it was you, Kurgan. I didn't even have to sense you...I could smell you from a mile away."

"MacLeod... I can't wait to wear that ponytail on my belt after I take your head!"

We rushed forward and slammed our sticks together. I pretended to give it my all, but made sure I broadcasted my moves. I didn't want to bust him in the knuckles or the face with my stick.

We somersaulted and twirled and finally the endgame was upon us.

I let Jeremy knock the sword from my hand. I went to my knees, because that's what you do when you lose a sword fight with another immortal. He stood on a stump next to the trail and held his sword out in front of him.

"There can be only one."

With that, he did his signature move. He jumped and twirled in midair. When he hit the ground he stumbled and almost fell over, but I steadied him with my hand. Then I went back to hanging my head in a manner fitting the soon-to-be executed.

He tapped the stick lightly against my neck and said, "Bink."

We laughed and started down the trail.

The portion of the trail we were on was lined with trees that hung over the middle and almost connected the two sides. It gave it a hidden path kind of feel that we both loved.

After walking a bit, I grew tired of listening to nothing but the bugs screeching around us.

"You learn any new songs on your thing?"

"Oh yeah, I almost forgot."

Jeremy pulled out his little red tin kazoo.

"You ever hear of the Violent Femmes?"

"No. That sounds like a girl band…is it?"

"Nah man, they have this really awesome song. My mom has it on cassette and I've been practicing all week."

He started playing "Blister in the Sun," and I still think his version of the song is the best I've ever heard.

We walked along the trail a ways, Jeremy playing his song and me kind of bopping my head along.

In the distance, we saw our prize.

We had heard stories that the trestle had been around since the civil war, back when the trail had been a train line. There was no proof whatsoever that any battles had been fought near it, but that didn't stop us from climbing down the slope next to it and wading in the creek looking for old cannonballs. The trestle was thirty-feet across and about twenty-feet of come-and-get-it to the creek below. We liked it because it didn't have any rails, and come late summer when the creek was deeper due to the rain and running fast, we held hour-long dare marathons to try to get each other to take the plunge.

As we were taking our shoes and socks off preparing to wade through the creek, Jeremy paused and looked like he remembered something really important that he forgot to do.

"Hey, did you mean what you said?"

"About what?"

"When you said Han would beat Indy? Do you really believe that?"

"Oh, man, sure I meant that. It's basically a fact."

"On what grounds?"

"On the grounds that Han is a space pirate and Indy is just a scientist. A cooler than average scientist, but he doesn't have a laser gun or a spaceship so he there's no way he could beat Han."

"But Indy's a pirate too."

"Not even, he just steals old junk from tombs and stuff. Not the same thing."

"He doesn't just steal any old stuff. He steals awesome stuff. Like the grail. And he goes on adventures to places that really exist, so maybe they could really happen. And he punches Nazis. He punches lots of Nazis."

We came to a unanimous consensus that punching Nazis was pretty cool.

We were up to our knees at that point, walking down the middle of the stream looking for cannon balls and rusty confederate bayonets when we heard an engine off in the distance slowly getting closer. We didn't pay it much mind at first, there was always someone riding around on four-wheelers on the trail, but then we heard rocks crunching as someone pulled off just before the trestle.

We waited a few minutes in silence. When nothing happened we went back to our hunt.

Something big enough to splash us from ten feet away hit the water with a crash.

We spun around. A T.V. was sitting half out of the water at a crooked angle. Two newly post-pubescent voices cackled. I put my hand up to shield my eyes and saw the last two people I ever wanted to catch me alone in the woods.

Ozak Biggs and Paden Thorn, both a few years ahead of us in age, and both a few behind us in mental development.

Ozak put his hand up to shield his eyes and pretended to see us for the first time.

"Oh shit, Paden, we got us a couple girls for company."

Paden laughed and spit tobacco juice into the air and it splattered in the water.

"Hey girls, why don't you come on up and hang out. Throw shit into the water with us."

Jeremy and I looked at each other. His eyes were moving faster than usual and his cheeks had a flushed look. He liked those two less than I did.

Being an easy target, he had a whole list of people he tried to steer clear of.

But, if we didn't go up there they would probably come down with us, and then they'd be mad.

We made our way out of the creek and climbed up the slope to the top of the trestle.

The pimple field on Ozak's face was covered in sweat, just like the seven or eight hairs on Paden's upper lip.

Ozak spit over the side and put his hand on his hip when we stood next to them.

"What were you ladies doing down there? Were you on a date? What you think Paden? Think these two are sweet on each other?"

"Seem to be. Looked pretty friendly down there. Were you two touchin' each other's pee pees before we showed up?"

Jeremy looked down at the water than back at Paden.

"We were just looking for some crawfish. You guys could come down and help us if you want."

Jeremy was a true pirate. He would never divulge our classified cannonball information to anyone.

"Hmph. Sounds about boring as hell. We brought some shit to break, you can do that with *us.*"

Paden walked over to his four-wheeler and pulled a black trash bag off the back. He opened the bag, pulled out a glass bottle and threw it down at the T.V. in the creek. A thousand shards of glass made acquaintance with the creek bed.

"Don't do that!"

Ozak stopped with his arm halfway in the black bag. He slowly pulled out a bottle.

"People walk in that creek. Lots of people and little kids, they come here in the summer and look for crawfish. They'll get hurt and cut up really bad if you keep breaking glass. Please stop."

Ever since the other kids we had grown up with learned to talk, they had picked on Jeremy. He had been bullied and bruised for so long that he was numb to violence. The fear was beaten out of him.

I, on the other hand, rarely got picked on. I was scared shitless and I was keeping my mouth shut, hoping that Jeremy wouldn't do anything to piss them off.

"Huh. Whatever you say your highness. Guess we got to find something else to do."

Paden gave Ozak a *you're gonna love this* look.

"Say, either of you boys seen titties yet?"

The heat coming off my face could have fried an egg.

We both shook our heads.

"Well you two are surely in for a treat. Ozak, show 'em that picture of your dad's girlfriend."

Ozak's lips separated and he showed us mossy, yellow teeth. He reached into his back pocket and pulled out a folded Polaroid. Paden gave Jeremy a nudge closer and Ozak pulled me into his musty orbit. He unfolded the picture.

A topless woman was straddling the arm of a couch, one hand holding a cigarette, the other holding one of her breasts.

I felt a burning in my chest I couldn't explain at the time.

"Shoot, those tits give me a boner every time. What you think four-eyes? Those give you some weird feelings in your crotch or what?"

Jeremy's eyes were oddly still. He looked up from the Polaroid and then at Ozak and Paden.

"I think you shouldn't be showing that to people. It isn't right."

Ozak and Paden looked at each other. They weren't smiling anymore. Ozak held the picture out in front of him so it was right in Jeremy's face.

"Now wait a second, we were being nice to you faggits by showing you these titties and this is how you repay us? By telling us we're not right?"

Paden took a step closer to Jeremy.

A golf ball formed in my throat and my hands were shaking. I wanted to say something, but I couldn't. Fear had me paralyzed in its tentacles. They were going to do something bad, and I couldn't move, not even for my best friend.

"Yeah, it's not right. That's somebody's daughter or somebody's sister. How do you think she would feel if she knew you were showing her picture to people? It's not right."

I don't think any of us were expecting Jeremy to grab the picture from Ozak's hand.

Ozak reached out and grabbed Jeremy by the wrist and tried to pry his fingers apart. Paden had a hold of Jeremy's arm and they were both shaking him around like a rag doll.

But he held on.

Paden lost his footing in the scuffle and tripped over his own feet to the side. I hadn't moved once. I was still in shock that Jeremy was brave enough to do that.

Now it was just Jeremy and Ozak tugging on the photo. Ozak had pried a corner of the Polaroid loose and was pulling it towards him when his hands slipped off.

And then Jeremy wasn't there anymore.

The only sound was the frogs and the crickets screaming at the heat. Paden looked at Ozak, then peered over the edge of the trestle. He looked back at Ozak and took off running for his four-wheeler. Ozak didn't even look. I heard him saying "shit" over and over again as he raced after Paden. The four-wheeler roared to life and I was left alone at the top of the trestle. I trudged through quicksand and looked over the edge.

Jeremy's feet were sticking up in the air to the right of the T.V. The rest of him was wedged into the creek bed.

I don't remember climbing down the slope, but when I got to the bottom my hands and arms were covered in scratches and blood.

Jeremy was sitting on the side of the creek with his feet in the water. His face and hair was covered in mud. His ponytail had come loose. He was coughing and shaking his head, one hand holding his chest. His other hand held his glasses, which were broken at the nose. He looked at me when I sat down beside him, though I know he couldn't see.

"My mom is going to kill me."

I didn't have anything to say to that.

I helped him to his feet and he held the two halves of his glasses up to his eyes. He looked up at the trestle.

"Did it look cool?"

"The coolest. It looked like Indy going after the grail."

He smiled and put his glasses in his pocket.

I put my arm through his and helped him back up to the trail.

Once on solid ground again, my arm now over his shoulder to help guide him, he pulled out his kazoo and played "Blister in the Sun" until we reached his trailer.

BETHANY FREESE is a writer who lives in the Pacific Northwest.

A TORONTO WHITETAIL

I went inside the wooden shed and saw a deer hanging stiff along the rafters, its legs like willowy branches, wrapped in husks of orange twine. I watched my father rip into its flesh, cutting and peeling off the pale skin.

I sat below watching the bloodied floor, the soft red stream, and I looked at my father's face, his thick pores sunken deep and hollow under the shed light, his eyes green but empty.

I watched his hands rinsing off the fur with a hose, cool sops of bloody water on my arms, neck, and lips, and I watched his thick red arms blending into the meat, laying the headless slab of flesh onto the table.

I watched his hands sharpening knives, the oil oozing and spiraling into the smooth charcoal. There was a rare calmness in his eyes, his skin the color of cod, his black hair almost gold under the glow of the light.

And then he made me cut the meat. My hands seeped into the cool flesh, cutting out long stocks and swaddling large clumps and wrapping them in paper, the meat bleeding from the sides.

He cut out the heart and laid it in a clear glass jar, his hands slapping the heart into the frying pan, glazed in fat and butter, sizzling as it slid back and forth. My father forced me to eat from his hands. I could feel the meat slipping down my throat, its flesh inside my own. I couldn't stop devouring it, filling me whole, filling me violently, with no licks of sauce or curds of cheese, but just the flesh inside me, the gamey taste of venison, the ripe meat.

D. A. GRAY spends his time as a full-time graduate student at Texas A&M University-Central Texas in the spring and fall, and as an MFA candidate at Sewanee School of Letters in the summer. Gray originally hails from Western Kentucky but, after retiring from the U.S. Army, now resides in Central Texas. Gray has published one book of poetry, *Overwatch*, Grey Sparrow Press, November 2011. His work can also be found in *Grey Sparrow Journal*, *Bellow*, *Poetry Salzburg* and *Spark: A Creative Anthology*.

NATURAL HISTORY

Across the hall diners gather trays and shuffle
toward the galley as if arrays of tables
were fences, and their march, one behind the other,
led to the feast of kings where pink meat steams

under yellow lamps, and here a dim light hangs
above a framed relief that, unobserved,
clings to a museum wall. Naked fluorescent bulbs
wash a picture of the hunt in a dull white glow

where early man thrusts his spear
into a bison's neck. Though the fight exists in paint,
a howling shines from the broad beast's eyes,
the flex of human jaw, a gleam of teeth.

Agony and survival have honed themselves to an edge
that pierces. Nothing and everything is beautiful.
A cloven hoof rising in an arc could kick a man to earth;
streaks of red connect the cunning to the flesh.

Blackness trowelled into the subject's lips
denotes a missing tooth. This first man lives
on the blunt end of a kill that happens again
each morning when the light flips on.

No weeks of feast or drink, nor huddling against the cold,
no limestone bed to wait for hunger's answer,
the telltale rumble of hooves, no sharpening or crouching
in tall grass, rubbing the aches of month-old scars—

only the piercing hangs across the hall from the cafe
with its folding resin tables. We, little kings, push back
bloated;
leaving only gristle on dirty plates. A busboy will scrape
remains into the trash while we stare back to the serving
line

as if to say, *kill me another*. And someone does.

COMPOST

Behind the Rhododendron lay the mound of each uneaten scrap,
a growing hill of refuse hidden behind eight foot of leaf towering above
yard and garden, red petals torn at their outer edges like confetti.

Some nights we walked with visitors to the end of the mower's path,
and at the edge marveled what limbs sagged beneath their weight
and when our company left

       one of us would carry the covered

plastic bowl, with fragrant cantaloupe rinds and collard stems,
peapods and potato skins, carrot greens and corn husks,
leaves of strawberries with the trace of white flesh clinging,
juice leaking from under the lid and onto the hands.

Gift in hand, we'd push back the flowering bush, dump dinner
waste onto a hill in the throes of rising, sinking, flower-heads
of Johnson grass, perfumed rot, a face full of flies.

Sometimes we think people hide their worst, until we've pushed
past heavy branches alone, where sacred myrrh lingers in drenched air,
found the red blossom, the death we're holding in our hands.

SHERI L. WRIGHT is a two-time Pushcart Prize and Kentucky Poet Laureate nominee and the author of six books of poetry, including the most recent, *The Feast of Erasure*. Wright's visual work has appeared in numerous journals, including *Blood Orange Review*, *Prick of the Spindle*, *Blood Lotus Journal* and *Subliminal Interiors*. In 2012, Ms. Wright was a contributor to the Sister Cities Project Lvlds: Creatively Linking Leeds and Louisville. Her photography has been shown across the Ohio Valley region and abroad. Currently, she is working on her first documentary film, *Tracking Fire*.

LAST OF THE DEER CLAN

The frogs do not sing to me anymore.
I listen to the conversations of owls like an intruder,
steal an intimacy that will never be shared.
Even the bones of my ancestors speak in tones
only the earth can hear and no longer whisper
their memories into my dreams.

I am left with the people of moon-colored skin
who bark at each other like angry dogs,
howl songs of whiskey and god,
ladle them both into their palms to hold at night
when all they have is the coldness of stars
that stare across the hours.

I watched all summer
and they thought me a fox
skimming the shadows of dusk
while they settled into their comfort,
children roosting in their laps.

One night, I stayed hidden in a curl of beargrass,
banked like embers, drawing warmth from
firelight diffused from a window so close
I could see amber beads pearled together on its surface.
And I reached out to touch the memory of a wife,
watched droplets trail down glass like a broken strand
into my palm
and disappear.

TRACY BIRD currently resides in Tampa, Florida. She completed her BA in English Literature and Creative Writing from the University of Arizona in 2007. She received recognition for excellence in both creative and academic writing there. Bird is an alumnus of the Eckerd College Writers Conference where she studied under Andre Dubus III. Her short story, "The Dress," was published in *Sabal* in 2013. Bird is currently living in Tampa, Florida, where she is blessed to have the support of her family in pursuing her writing full-time.

THEY EAT DOGS

My family is getting a divorce, no doubt about it. I know what happens in a divorce and first is a lot of fighting. Since summer started forty-two days ago, Mom and Dad have fought almost every day, and mostly about me.

"What about Amos?" Dad says.

"He's a kid. He'll be fine," Mom says.

My best friend Meeker is divorced and he told me all about when it happened to him. His mom told him nothing would change but Meeker hasn't seen his dad since summer before last. He still doesn't know exactly why his family got a divorce but I know mine has a reason: it's because I'm adopted. Mom told me about it, back when I was eight. She said "We'll talk about it when you're older."

Now I'm twelve and we still haven't talked about being adopted. I've never told anyone, not even Meeker. But today I'm on a mission to find out about being adopted. I started real early in my dad's office but I didn't find anything, not even my birth certificate, which I already know doesn't have the names of my real parents on it.

"Mom, why don't you tell me more about being adopted?" I say at breakfast.

"We chose you, out of all the little boys we could have had," she says. "That's all you need to know."

That's not much more than she told me when I was eight.

"But who else is adopted? Biscuit is the only other person I know who's adopted." Biscuit is our dog. He's my best friend outside of Meeker. We adopted him from the pound.

"It's not a big deal, Amos. You're just you. We wanted you. We picked you."

"How exactly do you go about picking a baby? Is there a place where you go and look at all the babies who are going to be adopted?"

"No. We picked you before you were born, when your natural mother decided to let you be adopted."

"So if you'd picked a different baby, who would I be?"

Mom rolls her eyes.

"Why didn't you just get a baby the way normal people do?"

"That reminds me, I have something for you," Mom says. "*The Boy's Guide to Growing Up.* I thought you might want to read it, now that you're turning thirteen and starting middle school." She gets up from the table.

"But I'm twelve," I tell her when she comes back with the book. "And middle school doesn't start for thirty-three days. What about being adopted?"

"There's nothing more to talk about," Mom says as she walks out of the kitchen. I pick up the book.

Puberty. That word even sounds gross. I know as soon as I open the cover that I can't be alone with this book. It's too gross. Me somewhere reading about puberty and Mom somewhere thinking I'm reading about puberty. So I put the book in my room and go out to look for Meeker.

.....

"What's an or-gas-m?" Meeker asks.

"Don't ask me. I didn't read it," I say. We're in my room. He's really into *The Boy's Guide to Growing Up*.

"Your Mom just gave it to you?"

"Yeah, she just gave it to me like it was *The Incredible Journey* or some other normal book like that. She said she thought I'd want to read it."

"Your Mom gave you porn. She's so cool," Meeker says. "Listen to this: 'After a boy and a girl go through puberty and they have intercourse—that means going all the way—they might conceive a child. This means that the girl can get pregnant and have a baby. This can happen even the first time they have intercourse. It is not necessary to have an—an—an or-gas-m for the girl to get pregnant'," Meeker reads. He looks at me again.

"So look it up," I say.

"'Orgasm,'" he reads from the dictionary. "''The human sexual response and release which, in the male, may include ejaculation. Climax.'"

I don't know what to say. It's so quiet in my room I can hear Meeker breathe.

"Hey—can I take the book to camp?" he says.

"Yeah. Just don't tell my Mom. Or your Mom," I say. Meeker's leaving for sleep-away camp tomorrow. I can't go because kids get molested at sleep-away camp, according to Mom.

"He's only twelve,"she said.

"Thirteen," Dad said, even though I won't be thirteen until November. But I still can't go.

.....

"Does the beach close at a certain time?" I ask. Mom and Dad are in the front seat but no one answers. We're having a quality time day. We're supposed to be going to the beach but instead we are waiting maybe forever in line for gas.

Across Memorial Drive from where we're parked people are marching up and down the sidewalk, some waving their arms, some carrying big black-and-white signs: "Send the Shah Back." "Leave Iran to the Iranians." I can hear their loud voices but I can't tell what they're yelling.

"Dad, what's a shah?"

No answer.

"Ninety-three degrees in Metro Houston today," the announcer on the radio says. To save gas we are sitting in the Buick with the windows rolled down and no air conditioning. Next to me on the back seat, Biscuit pants and slobber drips from his tongue onto the plastic seat covers.

"Two hours," Dad says. "We're still not near the station." There's a line of cars in front of us and a line of cars behind us.

"Amos, do you know why we can't get gas?" Dad asks. "Let me teach you something. Two years ago our president told those *A*-rabs—"

"Don't say that," Mom says. "Call them by the proper name."

"Sand n—"

"Don't you dare, Ray."

"Kidding, Beth. Guess you're becoming a liberal now that you hang out with that hippie friend of yours."

Mom's hippie friend is Mary. She wears her hair in two long braids, and she has a tattoo of a peace symbol on her arm.

"Ray, don't say that. Why do you have to label everyone?"

"Anyway, the question is why can't we get gas?"

"Because those guys in Arabia—" I say.

"Saudi Arabia," Mom says. "But you're wrong. It's because of the revolution, in Iran."

"—won't give us any," I finish.

"Wrong." Dad makes a honking sound through his nose like the buzzer on The Price is Right. "It's because the world does not take one James Earl "Jimmy" Carter seriously. Two years ago Mr. Carter told all the big players in the Middle East that refusing to free up oil during an energy crisis is the moral equivalent of war against the U.S. of A., Amos. We're going to keep going through this unless something changes. We need to show them just what we can do to get the oil flowing. We have the ammo, the means of delivery, and a damn good reason for doing it."

Dad starts the car and we move forward a couple of feet then stop.

"For doing what?" I ask.

"Ray, don't."

"Nuking the bastards," Dad says.

"This is 1979, not the Dark Ages. We should know better. Maybe Jimmy Carter knows better."

"Thank you, flower child, for the history lesson."

"Ray, open the trunk," Mom says. She must want more wine from the cooler she packed for the beach. She's drinking from one of my Star Wars Slurpee Collector Cups.

She put Luke's head on Darth Vader's body and she's drinking from Luke's head with a straw.

"Why didn't you get gas yesterday?" she says as she climbs back into the car with her full cup. Just then the cars in front of us start leaving the line and driving away.

"They don't have any gas, Ray."

"Anyone up for ice cream?" Dad says.

....

It's the same day, and we're back at our house. Surprise, Mom and Dad are fighting. All afternoon they've been going at it.

Dad says, "It seems to me that you've already made up your mind. No doubt with some help from Mary."

"I know that's what you think, but just because you say it doesn't make it true. And you still haven't told me what you want."

"Gee," Dad says, "what do I want? I want a clean house and a wife who isn't soused half the time. I want to live in the same house as my wife and kid. Hell, I even want that stupid dog that pisses on my pant cuffs." Biscuit has a thing for Dad's work pants. "I want a nice life in *my* nice house. I want to swim in *my* nice pool in *my* nice back yard."

It seems like Dad comes home later every night. And he works on Saturday and Sunday, except for quality time days like today, I guess.

.....

"Dad, can we talk about being adopted?" I say between bites of my TV dinner. They've stuck me in the living room with a TV tray and turned on "Wonderful World of

Disney." I can hear them fighting because the dining room is right next door but they don't seem to hear me.

"Dad." I yell this time.

"What?"

"Can we talk about being adopted? I don't even know anyone who's adopted but Biscuit." I want to know what would have happened to Biscuit if nobody picked him or to me if nobody picked me. I might live in Wisconsin or Mexico or in an orphanage. I might be having more fun.

"Later," he says for about the gillionth time.

I think I'm too old for "Wonderful World of Disney."

.....

Ten more days until Meeker comes home. There's nothing for me to do but watch the new neighbors and hang out with Mom and Mary. Yesterday I heard Mom say she's waiting for Dad to leave, so she can keep this house.

"I love this house," she said.

"Possession is nine-tenths of the law," Mary said.

"I love this subdivision."

Our subdivision is called Sherwood Forest and all the streets have names like Robin Hood Lane and Friar Tuck Circle. Our house is in the Oak Tree style with the chocolate color scheme, Mom says. Down at the end of our subdivision they're still building houses. Kids from the middle school and high school go down there to smoke pot and fool around, according to Meeker's older brother, Chad.

"Mary, did it hurt to get your tattoo?" I say.

"It hurt a lot, and I have to wear long sleeves at work all the time, so no one will see it. Especially the kids." Mary works at the middle school, in the office. My middle school.

"Good thing you don't have to work in the summer. Do you know anyone who's adopted? Other than me."

"Sure. Jesus. And John Lennon," Mary says.

"But Jesus still had his real mother."

"I'm your real mother, Amos. The one who feeds you and loves you and helps you with your homework." She sounds the way she sounds when I'm in trouble.

"And John Lennon has a peace symbol tattoo too," Mary says.

"Why don't you go for a swim, Amos," Mom says. It doesn't sound like a question so I jump in the water and practice holding my breath. I can listen to Mom and Mary when I come up for air.

"You're a free spirit, Beth. Just like me. You should be in an open marriage, or not married at all. Ray and his narrow mind are sucking the life out of you."

"I know you're right. That's why I told him to leave." She told Dad to leave? When?

"What about Amos?" Mary says.

"Amos is good. I mean he's a kid. He doesn't have any idea." I imagine Mom looking over at me so I put my face in the water but not my ears.

"Hey, Amos," Mom calls. I stay real still so she'll think I can't hear her.

"Amos, it's four o'clock—go check the mail." She wants me to leave so she can smoke one of Mary's cigarettes. Like I don't know she smokes. I've even seen her do it. In my room, one of the windows looks right over the pool and that's where they smoke. The other window looks right at the new neighbor's house. They have a daughter. Mom told me her name is Su Lin. She's a stone cold fox. I watched her help her parents move a pink couch into the house yesterday. She doesn't know I've been watching her because you can't see into my room through that window. I checked once, when I was ten, and the Camerons lived next door.

When I go through the side gate to get the mail, Su Lin is standing right in front of me, watering flowers by the side of her house. When she sees me she smiles and sets down the hose. Then she stands up and motions for me to follow her, so I do.

Her garage is cool and dark after the hot July sun and I can't see for a second but then Su Lin is in front of me again, wearing cut-off jeans and a yellow bikini top. The garage walls are lined with neat stacks of boxes. Su Lin pulls a magazine from a box that stands alone with its flaps hanging open. I can see the cover: it's a Playboy. I've heard about Playboy from Meeker's older brother but I've never seen one.

Su Lin still hasn't said a word. Maybe she doesn't speak English. I feel nervous.

"Are your parent's home?" I say slowly and a little loudly. She shakes her head no and sits on the little stoop that goes up to the kitchen door, just like the one at my house. She scoots over so I can sit next to her.

My swimsuit is cool and sticky against my skin. Su Lin arranges the magazine on her knees and opens it to the first page. The she starts turning the pages one by one. She scoots a little closer so I can see better.

The first dirty picture we come to is of a lady with blonde hair on her head and blonde hair down there too. Su Lin turns the page and there is a picture of only boobs on one page and writing on the other. The next page has a girl who is dancing. She is wearing a bra and knee socks on but no panties. Then Su Lin offers me the magazine and I move it to my knees. I continue turning pages one at a time, only faster. I'm praying there are more pictures when I find a page that folds out. I turn the magazine around so we can see the whole thing. This lady's boobs are bigger than the other lady's. She looks very tan or maybe she is just that color. She has long black hair.

My penis twitches in my swimming suit when I realize this woman looks like Su Lin. The lady's hair down there looks shiny, just like the hair on Su Lin's head. My penis is getting hard. I glance at Su Lin and she is smiling. She is watching me. What does she want? Why doesn't she talk? I'm still holding the magazine when she puts her hand on my leg, right up by my knee. I can't breathe and I can feel my penis standing up. Su Lin still has her hand on my knee when I start to shake. I know what's going to happen. I can't keep my eyes open when I feel it. It's different than when I make it happen, more in my stomach. Then it's over. I look at Su Lin and she is still smiling and I know she knows. I jump up so the magazine falls to the garage floor and I run.

When I get back to the pool, Mom and Mary have finished their cigarettes. Everything is the same as when I left, as if the whole world stopped and it's starting again now. I run straight to the pool and jump in. I open my eyes to watch the silver bubbles from my splash race to the top and vanish like the stars do when the Millennium Falcon enters hyperspace. When I come up for air Mom asks where the mail is. "There isn't any," I lie. I take a breath and sink to the bottom of the pool again.

.....

Two hours later I'm sitting at the dining room table waiting for dinner. Dad isn't home, as usual. Biscuit is waiting for me to sneak him some food. Out the dining room window I can watch Su Lin mowing the lawn in the same pair of cut-offs and the yellow bikini top.

"So'd you read the book I gave you?" Mom asks as she carries our TV dinners to the table.

"Mom, we're eating," I say. It's been eleven days since Meeker left for camp and Mom still doesn't know I gave the book to him.

"I think this is a good time to talk about it. I've seen you looking at Su Lin."

"I'm not hungry," I say. "May I be excused?"

"Fine, don't eat. But I expect you to sit here with me and have a nice dinnertime conversation." I can tell she's angry because she says "shit" when she knocks over her glass of wine.

"About what?" Biscuit nudges my leg from his spot under the table. When Mom looks away I give him a green bean.

"See, you are hungry," Mom says. "Tell me about what you learned in the book."

The dining room window is behind Mom's head. Su Lin marches toward us pushing the lawnmower.

"Amos?" Mom says.

"Uhm," I say. "Some words."

"Like what?"

I kind of wish my Dad was here. "Uh, testicles...origami...vagina."

"Orgasm," Mom says.

"Yeah. Orgasm. You don't have to have one to get a girl pregnant, you know." Su Lin turns the lawn mower around. Her blue-black hair hangs down her back like a horse's tail.

"Why can't we talk about being adopted?" I say because I know that will shut Mom up.

"They eat dogs, you know."

"Who?" I say.

"Koreans. The new neighbors are Korean," Mom says.

"How can you say that?"

"It's true," Mom says. "They eat dogs in Korea, and in Viet Nam, too."

I slip Biscuit a piece of chicken.

"I don't believe you," I say.

"Well, ask them. Just be polite about it. Stop staring out the window."

Su Lin turns the mower off and it's suddenly quiet in the dining room.

"She's beautiful. She's older than you. Fifteen," Mom says.

"I'm thirteen."

"Twelve," Mom says.

My face feels hot. "I don't believe you about the dogs," I say. It comes out really loud. "And I'm not going to ask them if it's true. I don't want to talk about them anymore. May I be excused?"

Biscuit follows me up the stairs to my room.

.....

Dad is coming to get his stuff today so I have to stay around the house and help him. Not that there's anything to do anyway.

As soon as he arrives Mom stomps up the stairs to their bedroom and slams the door. Earlier she moved all Dad's clothes into the hallway. Then she changed her mind and threw them all over the banister into the family room.

The U-Haul truck is orange and white. Me helping Dad is mostly me following behind him as he carries heavy boxes of books and other stuff up the ramp into the truck.

"When will Meeker be home from camp?" Dad says.

"One week from today, next Sunday. Dad, is Mary a hippie because she has a tattoo?" Dad is pushing his Lazy Boy recliner up the ramp.

"She has a tattoo?"

"Yeah, a peace sign. On the part of her arm above her elbow. She has to cover it up when she's at work."

"Well, I'd expect so. Taxpayer money pays her salary."

"Is that what makes her a hippie?"

"No. She's a hippie because she thinks the world should be one big happy place. Everything is peace and love with those people."

"Will Mom get a tattoo, now that they're friends?"

"If she does, she'll see me in court and she won't see much of you, Sport." Dad hasn't called me Sport since I was ten.

"What's an open marriage?"

"Christ," Dad says. "Is that what your Mom and Mary talk about?"

I follow Dad back into the house.

"Mary says Jesus was adopted. And John Lennon."

"She told you that? John Lennon is like the king of the hippies. Don't listen to her."

"Why am I adopted? Why didn't you have your own kid?"

"You're our own kid, Sport. Just don't think about it."

Dad picks up a box and starts putting his clothes in it. "You're just a little boy. We'll talk about it when you're older."

Dad tapes up the box and carries it outside.

"So where do you live?"

"In an apartment near the Galleria," Dad says.

"Can I go there with you tonight?"

"Not tonight, Sport, but soon."

"What's your phone number? Will you write it on the pad by the phone please?"

"I don't have one at home yet but you can call me at the office," Dad says.

But I know what happens when I call him at the office: he's always with a client or in court or out to lunch. "Or with some other woman," I heard Mom tell Mary once.

"How about the new neighbors?" Dad says. "Have you met them?"

"Oh, I see them around," I say.

"Has Mom met them?"

"I guess so. The daughter is Su Lin. She's fifteen. They're Korean. Mom says they eat dogs, Koreans. Do they?"

"They might in their country. Lots of people in this world'd be happy to eat dog, all those third world people."

Biscuit comes out of the house and follows me and Dad up the ramp into the truck. He climbs up on Dad's chair and curls up.

"Mom's been crying ever since you went to your apartment," I say.

"Your mother will get better now that she's getting what she wants. She thinks she's unhappy," Dad says. Then he laughs.

"But why?" I say.

"Maybe because you are all grown up," Dad says. "She doesn't know what to do when she's not being your mother. Or my wife."

"You just said I'm a little boy. I'm only thirteen. And she'll always be my Mom."

"Twelve," Dad says. "And trust me—pretty soon you won't be talking to your mother about everything."

He pulls down the door on the back of the truck.

.....

Dad's gone. It's really late and dark and Biscuit isn't home. Sometimes he wanders off but he always comes home for his dinner.

I'm going out to look for him.

There are puddles of June bugs under the street lights. Meeker says June bugs smell like hot buttered popcorn when you smash them. They tickle my feet when I step on them but I don't smell anything. Mom doesn't know I'm out with no shoes on. She doesn't know I'm out at all. I'm going down to the end of our subdivision, where the woods and the unfinished houses are. Biscuit goes down there sometimes.

I'm getting to the place where there aren't any sidewalks. Or streetlights, either, but I never noticed that when I'm down here in the daytime. I have Dad's big silver flashlight from his workbench and I turn it on.

"Biscuit." I yell as loud as I can.

If Mom tried to come looking for me, she'd miss every clue: the flashlight, my shoes. She didn't answer when I knocked on her bedroom door and I knocked for a long time. So I decided, hey, I'm almost thirteen. Old enough to walk alone at night. Old enough to find Biscuit.

"Biscuit." Nothing but my voice.

At first when I couldn't find Biscuit I thought he was in the house but I checked, even in the closets and under the stairs. I couldn't look in Mom and Dad's room because the door was locked. I went outside and called him every commercial during *Wild Kingdom* and *Battlestar Galactica*. I knocked on Mom's door and told her what was wrong but she wouldn't come out.

If Dad was here he'd know where to look for Biscuit.

I'm all the way down by the empty houses now, where the middle school kids come to smoke and drink and make-out. Maybe Biscuit is in one of the houses. I found him down here two days ago, in the woods at the end of the street. He keeps wandering off. I think he's looking for Dad.

I have to shine the flashlight on the ground now so that I don't step on any nails or glass.

"Biscuit." I yell really loud.

The unfinished houses are kind of scary in the dark; some have walls but no roofs, or glass in the windows but no doors. Some have almost everything.

"Biscuit?" I hear something in the fourth house on the street, like something is moving around. The house has glass in the windows but no front door. My voice echoes off the cement floors. I hear something for sure.

"Biscuit?"

I hear a sound like someone saying "shit" in a whisper. Or maybe it's Biscuit snuffling around in the dark.

"Biscuit?"

"Shh."

I know it's a voice this time.

"Biscuit, buddy, come on." I climb up on the cement foundation of the house. Biscuit's not on the first floor and I can't see up the stairs to the second floor, even with the flashlight. And then the flashlight goes out. Shaking it doesn't help so I climb the stairs in the dark.

"Biscuit! Come on!" I yell. I'm getting real scared now but I stop and I'm quiet, waiting and listening for Biscuit or whoever it is. When I get to the top step I can see the wood marking out bedrooms and hallways. There's something moving in one of the bedrooms but I'm not sure what I'm seeing. Then the moon comes out and shines through the window and I understand: in front of me, in the moonlight, is some guy's naked butt moving up and down and up and down. I can see Su Lin on the floor underneath the guy, who turns toward me and laughs.

"Hey, little buddy," he says.

I turn around so fast that I run into the plywood framing of the hall. Behind me I can hear the guy laughing, then Su Lin calls, "Come back, little boy. It's okay, little boy."

So she can speak English.

"I'm not a little boy," I yell. I take the last four stairs in one big jump.

.....

"I'll deal with you tomorrow," Mom says, when I walk through the door. Dad's car is in the driveway and Biscuit is in his favorite spot on the couch. "Where have you been with no shoes on?"

"I was looking for my dog." I can tell Mom and Dad have been arguing because her face is red and Dad's lips are in a straight line.

"He took a ride in my U-Haul, Sport. I couldn't bring him home until I finished unloading the truck. And I couldn't call because—"

"—you don't have a phone," I finish. "You told me."

"Amos, go to your room so your father and I can talk." Mom's voice is scratchy. Biscuit gets off the couch and follows me upstairs to the landing where I sit and listen.

"I'm not a criminal, Beth," Dad says. "What if there's an emergency, like what happened tonight, and I need to get into the house? And you'd best stop leaving the garage door unlocked, now that you're a woman living alone." Alone? What about me? She has me, and Biscuit.

"The papers say you are to give me the keys," Mom says.

"For hell's sake—I pay the mortgage on this house. I thought we could keep this civil. Here. Take your keys. I'll go."

"No Daddy, wait," I call out. "Please, Dad, I want to go with you."

"I'll see you next weekend. You know I have to work."

"I want to know where you live." I'm crying like a little kid. "Don't leave me here."

"This is your home, Sport. Your mother needs you here."

"Yeah. Just to clean the pool," I say. "I'm in trouble for leaving the house to look for Biscuit but Mom didn't even notice I was gone until I came home."

"That's not true," Mom says but she's lying. I told her Biscuit was missing. I knocked on her door. But I'm not going to tattle on her.

Dad gives me a high five. Mom doesn't say anything to him. Maybe she thinks I shouldn't love Dad anymore. But Mom's the one who's not the same. Most of the time she's trying to get rid of me, saying "go play, Amos." "Check the mail, Amos." She tells me she needs alone time. She doesn't notice that makes me alone, too.

Meeker never told me being divorced is so much trouble.

.....

It's ten in the morning and Mary comes walking through the back gate like she lives here.

"You got the job," she says to Mom.

"What job?" I say. I didn't even know Mom wanted a job.

"At the school," Mary says.

"What job? What school?"

"Your school. The middle school. I'll be working in the office with Mary," Mom says.

My mom working at my school? Like everything isn't bad enough already. Lots of kids know her. It might have been cool in elementary school where you go to the nurse when you're sick. You could go to your Mom instead. But middle school? They probably don't even have a nurse in middle school.

Through our fence I can see Su Lin, sitting in a chair in her backyard. She's wearing both pieces of the yellow bikini. I know she can hear every word we say.

"Why would you get a job at my school, Mom? You're such an idiot."

"Amos." Mom is using her warning voice.

"No, it's true. You don't care what I want," I say. "You smoke and drink with your friends because you think it makes you cool, just like some stupid kid. But you aren't cool. You're just old," I yell. "I know, I know, go to your room, Amos. Well, I'm not. I'm part of this family too. Why doesn't anyone ask what I want?"

Mom looks at me then gets up and goes into the house. She tries to slam the screen door behind her but it just bounces and hardly makes any noise.

"You're the man of the house now," Mary says. "Go check on your mom."

.....

Meeker's finally home. He comes over on Monday. We're sitting outside on the grass in my front yard. Meeker's hair is blonde and his face is all red from being out in the sun for three weeks.

"So, how was camp?" I say.

"Okay. I lost the book. The guys were passing it around and the counselor found it and took it away. He said he gave it back to me but he didn't."

"Oh well, don't tell my mom. Or your mom."

"Okay."

"Hey, I'm adopted, you know."

"For real?"

"Yeah, my mom told me a long time ago."

"Oh. That's cool. I wish I was adopted."

"Why?" I say.

"My dad. I could have had a different dad."

"My dad never came for me on the weekend," I say. "I waited the whole time. Mom says I must be confused about him coming. He hasn't called me, either. And I know what he told me."

Meeker nods his head; he knows all about this stuff.

"Seems like all my mom does since he left is smoke and drink wine or whatever," I say. "Mary's always here. Mom knows I know she smokes now and she doesn't care."

"Yeah. Well. I'm glad my dad's gone. No more hitting," Meeker says.

"Yeah," I say.

Just then Su Lin comes out of her house wearing those cut-off jeans and a halter top. Meeker looks at her.

"Uhm," he says.

"Yeah," I say. "She's real pretty, but, you know, they eat dogs."

JASMINE V. BAILEY's poems have appeared in *32 Poems, Cimarron Review, Verse Daily,* and *Crab Orchard Review,* among other journals. Her chapbook, *Sleep and What Precedes It,* is available from Longleaf Press, and her book-length collection, *Alexandria,* is available from Carnegie Mellon University Press.

ELEGY WITH AFRICA

All summer we waited for night to fall—
first drinking, then dinner, and then the sweet release
from each other in sleep, in dreams we walked
circling lives we couldn't locate. Not until you left
did the daylight relent, and then night marooned me
between useless curtains, looking out.
You Barishnikoved through our dreamt-of theaters.
New York pulled storms into it and swept them away
before I felt I had them, and as they departed,
the sick half-light painted a clear, if bruised picture
of one of the views I had prayed for and been given.

•

They've given the richest continent to thieves
who water the unstoppable desert with blood.
Who court immortality in Lincolns, flirting
with the gods that are never full on goats.
In hunger, the markets were strung up with monkeys
with pathetic faces and the lines for medicine
grew so long they became an independent occasion
for death. In each collapse, a heap of bright linen.
The sky watches all this and grows enamored
of the first good man she sees. She wishes for arms, fearing
he will not discover the new meaning of rain.

•

The apartment with too many bedrooms mocks
every emptiness you knew. With no one to waste money
on flowers, the tables grow infinite. Set a wine glass
here—later you will move it to the sink or carry it
upstairs. Africa wraps the Sahara around its shoulders
and grows no warmer, you read the books he took out
from the library on Alma Thomas, he read
half of *Spring Snow* and neither of you grew softer.
When the snow arrived, far from teasing
an early spring, it cut the ribbon of a fathomless winter
that originated in your body. The cold bled
through your feet into the tectonic plates, the ocean
swelled and a shudder crept up the spine of Japan.
You stand in a line you will never reach the front of,
your hand out, your legs buckling, wanting to recover less
than to receive the pardon that ends the nightmare
of sudden and gradual disappearance.

MEDEA

I did not expect the day to end in dawn,
or the river in the photograph to flood

the living room. But I expected to see you
again: upright, studied. Wearing your summer

of meat in the Azores and pelagic freedom.
Instead you haunt Van Ness,

crossing the stone bridge invisible where
a girl jumped from it thinking of her grandfather.

More than one ghost can play
your tortured Jesuit tune. In Paris

they sell themselves on straw mattresses,
buy brandy, live on regret

as the rich live on fashion.
The mice eat the feathers in their hair

when they lie under windows remembering sleep.

Holy candles burn a day and a half, lit with coins
needed for other things. The gods

feast on women's misery, paying out
promises. They rarely wake from their clouds

to take up lorgnettes
and tell the world what they were dreaming,

which someone will call writ, another
thunder. I recognize your voice in their nonsense,

sweeter than being young or right.

LORETTA DIANE WALKER is a two-time Pushcart nominee. She has published two collections of poetry. Her manuscript *Word Ghetto* won the 2011 Bluelight Press Book Award. Walker's work has appeared in a number of publications, including *The Concho River Review*, *Haight-Ashbury Literary Journal*, *Illya's Honey*, *Orbis International Journal*, *San Pedro River Review*, *The Texas Observer,* and *94 Creations*. She teaches music at Reagan Magnet School in Odessa, Texas. Loretta received a BME from Texas Tech University and earned an MA from The University of Texas of the Permian Basin.

TO A BROKE POET

There's not much difference between star and stone
in the hard sky of need.
Stones can be dealt, but who can shuffle or cut a star?
Can the fat tale of a comet fill an empty stomach
or even odds? Ask the broke poet
who tries to stuff the Milky Way in the cup
of her obsession; she is driven by need to tempt the decks.
This image junky stares at the moon,
sees an eye bulging from the socket of night,
depends on words and constellations to feed her fix.

She reads messages in the wind, swears
the breeze bru—shhhh, brush, brushing against the window
is the sharp elbow of the earth
prodding, prompting her to bet everything
she doesn't own. Love or luck makes her believe
air and the plump voices of morning
are hers to wager.

Once she slid an ace of diamonds
in the ribs of her poems, then sat at the blackjack table.
Her face was as intimidating as a blank sheet of paper.
She stacked metaphors like poker chips,
dared the dealer to challenge them.
She tapped the table with her BIC
as though the odds were in the pen.
Hit me. Again. Again. Again.
When the last card busted her hand,
she dropped the ace on the stack,

broke into a smile, then walked away humming
with the breeze bru—shhhh, brush, brushing against the
window.

BRIANNE KOHL's short stories have appeared in *Black Heart Magazine*, *Ohio Edit*, *Crack the Spine Literary Magazine*, *The Corner Club Press*, *The Bohemyth*, *Epiphany Magazine*, *See Spot Run*, *The Foghorn*, *Independent Ink*, and *The Masters Review: New Voices*. She has work anthologized in *Crack The Spine Fall 2013* and *Spark: A Creative Anthology*. Kohl has fiction forthcoming from *The Stoneslide Corrective*.

CHASING THE CRACKS

She felt a sharp pull towards her father's abandoned wine cellar, bottles stacked nice and gathering a thick film of dust. She felt the drag in her throat—such a thirsty magnetism. But Jenna settled for tea instead. Peppermint green tea, piping hot with no sugar, no cream. It soothed her sick stomach. She convinced herself it was ceremonial. A comforting ritual, her father, Bobby, would say as if it were some loyalty to sacrament to only have loose leaf tea in the house. But, he'd given up the booze and he liked to say that he needed those modest comforts.

"Wine is an investment," she remembered him telling her on her eighteenth birthday. His breath had been sour and he'd misjudged the distance between them. His grape teeth and shadowed lips kissed at her cheek like a baby's mouth, gaping open and messy as it brushed against her skin. "Good wine is always an investment. Your mama taught me that."

He'd fallen down the stairs that night. Clean down, hitting his back against the treads. She'd spent the last few hours of her birthday in a hygienically white waiting room. She'd sat, alone—a little drunk, herself—wondering how the night would have gone had he had broken his neck instead of his arm.

"Where's Mike tonight?" he asked Jenna. Her back muscles coiled tight. She had a tremor she couldn't shake, spreading out from her throat all the way to her finger tips. She felt like a snake caught in a partial shed, itchy and myopic. He asked it casually—the kind of question you ask while searching for your keys or flipping through the channels. But, she'd been expecting it and chewed it around, looking for the fat.

"Had to work late tonight," she finally answered and pretended to sip her tea. Steam rose up past her face and fogged her glasses. The heat radiating through the porcelain burnt her fingers a little, but she didn't want to put it down. She pulled the mug into her chest to hide the tremor in her hands.

"He's been working a lot of extra hours lately," Bobby replied. His tea was left untended on the little table beside his chair, steam floating up like a wispy ghost.

"He likes to work," Jenna said.

"Hmm," Bobby replied and frowned at her. There it is, Jenna thought. The fat of it. Some morsel of gristle he could chew on until all she had left were her bones.

"I should get going," she said and pushed her feet into the thick white carpet. She looked around for her shoes, although she knew they were tucked neat beside the front door. She'd kicked them off when she'd entered the foyer but he'd trotted along behind her, mating them into an ordered pair.

"So soon?" he asked. "I feel like you just got here. Feels like I never get to spend time with my little girl anymore."

"I'm hardly a little girl," Jenna said and stood. She felt a little dizzy as she straightened and winced at a sharp cramp in her stomach. Normal pains, the books had said. Welcome them. Her body was working without her, creating a safe place for those tiny recklessly dividing cells —so needful of a private garden to grow.

"You'll always be my little girl, Jenna-bear," he said and smiled. She felt like she was looking at him through a wall of ice. "Well, wait!" he said then, excited. "I forgot, I have something for you."

Jenna moved closer to the foyer but waited as her father ran up the curved stair case. She could hear him open a dresser drawer, slam it shut. She tracked his footsteps across the ceiling until he reappeared, skipping down the steps.

She imagined the way his feet had slid out from beneath him once. She loved her father. Truly. But he was a phantom pain, a severed limb she'd learned to live without early on. This new father—the one that called her all the time, the one that begged her to come over, see him, see how well he was doing—was too attentively prosthetic.

"Here," he said and held out a hand. In his palm was a small opal pendant spun on a square platinum chain. It was delicate, the kind of chain that tangles into knots. Fire was trapped in the pendant, sparkling in the light from the gaudy crystal chandelier eighteen feet above. "It was your mother's."

She looked up at him, her eyes quick and narrowed. "Why are you giving it to me?"

"Because, I think she'd want you to have it," he answered and slid it into her open palm. She watched her own fingers spasm around it.

"I don't want it," she said and tried to give it back.

Bobby made a distressed sound in the back of his throat, a huff of disappointment. "Jenna, don't be like that. Your mother was a good woman."

A good woman, Jenna repeated in her head. *Whatever that's worth.* She stuffed the opal necklace into her pocket and vowed to store it away as soon as she got home.

"You've been acting off lately, Jenna," Bobby said. "I can't put my finger on it." Jenna shifted away from him, tugging at the sleeves of her oversized sweatshirt. Men see what they can afford to see, she thought. Nothing more. She slipped on her shoes.

"I have to go, Dad," she said and left him standing alone at the door. As she walked to her car, the wind swept clouds over the setting sun and yanked at the branches of the Black Walnut trees. Her old tire swing dangled from the tree closest to the garage. It thudded in a steady rhythm against the dull white wall. Why hadn't he pulled it down? It was a sad reminder of happy summers. A happiness, so hot and primitive. Before autumn had set in.

With her hand poised on her open car door, Jenna stared at the front of the house. Growing up, it had been a wild thing—overgrown and lush. The yard had been all weeds and little white and yellow flowers. But, her father was a gardener now, caring for the thick manicured bushes and Creeping Wild Rye grass. Weeds were stamped out, burned away with chemicals. The lawn was mowed in perfect lines like a chess board. Jenna couldn't see it—how clean the house had become. All she saw was a memory: her mother sitting on the porch, hair gone crazy and a sweaty wine glass in her hand as she laughed at the heat of the summer.

Her mother had had the kind of laugh that used all of the muscles in her stomach. The kind that turned heads and made Jenna's chest ache with the love of it. Laughter like a Dandelion puff that blows across the yard. Love-in-a-puff, tiny white flowers and chartreuse seed pods implanting themselves into the cracks of the walkway. Her mother would laugh and yell out, "Step on a crack, break your mother's back!" as Jenna hopscotched her way up to the porch.

Jenna climbed into her car, started the engine and thought briefly of the new tires she needed. Just one more project Mike hadn't gotten to and maybe never would. She could see her father's silhouette in the kitchen window. Was he sad, she wondered. Now that he had begun to feel again? Did he regret? She thought of her liquor cabinet at home—colorful bottles in all shapes and sizes. She longed for that flare of heat from a smooth gin—that piney rend at her throat.

For so long it had distilled her, separated the volatility of her past from the way her life could boil up without her. As she drove, she stared at the windshield, barely seeing the yellow double lines in front of her. Her hands moved by rote, turning the wheel in blind movements.

She wouldn't give it up for her father. She needed that otherness, that altered light. He'd given her that dryness in her throat and now he wanted to take it away. He'd taken so many things away from her and now he was fine. Just fine and orderly like a pair of mated shoes.

She'd never given it up for Mike, not when he'd begged, not when he left. But this was after, now. Was her body even her own anymore? Her breasts, so sore. That queasy feeling that lasted all day: a sickness that left her mourning the loss of that altered light. What could she do? What *would* she do? How far could she take this?

Jenna tried to think of her mother, of the good times, the gin times, the laughing vodka tonic days. Those parties and the way they'd let her stay up late, watching the beautiful women, barely clothed. Running, giggling, from the men with their pinching fingers and winking eyes. But all those memories were overshadowed by that one moment. It only takes a moment for the party to end.

They'd been driving down this same road, her mother crying, sloshing over the rim of her favorite road mug. Her mother's cries had echoed around the old car, fresh cries of pain and warning. Tears fell from Jenna's eyes, but they belonged to her mother.

As the road passed in a blur, Jenna looked at the passenger seat and saw herself as she had been on that night. Her light blond hair had dandelion-yellowed from the sun and her pretty blue dress had black smudges on her back end from the tire swing. As a little girl, she'd gazed out the passenger window and listened to her mother cry.

". . . and one day you'll wonder, darlin'," her mother had said in between sobs. "You'll wonder where your husband went. He'll be gone because he never loved you enough. No matter how good you were to him, little girl, he'll have somebody else. You'll find him, in your own kitchen, with someone else. Because, there is always someone else. Somebody prettier . . ."

The car drifted left of center and Jenna pulled it back to the right, easing off the shoulder and skimming low hanging tree branches. From far off, Jenna heard cars honking and lights flashing. But, she didn't look behind her in the rear view mirror, she looked to her right and saw a scared yellow-haired child in a dirty dress. The little girl cried giant tears, "Where's Daddy. I want Daddy."

"Daddy is gone," Jenna told the child.

And then her head cracked into the windshield and the little girl flew free from the car, through the glass and landed on the hard moon-burnt shoulder. Tires screeched and angry metal rubbed against itself—the sound bit into her head as light flashed behind her brown eyes. The car stopped and Jenna flew back in her seat.

Bright dots of light erupted and faded like a firecracker popping inside her head. *A good woman*, her father had said. Her mother had been a good woman. Jenna was a good woman. But, really, what was a good woman worth?

Jenna leaned forward as far as she could and traced her index finger along the sharp edges of the spidery lines in the glass. A bright streetlight flickered above her, reflecting her mother's image into the broken pane. Jenna could feel where her mother's head had smashed into the glass on that day so long ago. When the world had been wild.

She followed those lines, hoping to find her mother and praying it wasn't her own reflection looking back at her.

She sat in her car, chasing the invisible cracks. Her car, resting safely on the soft shoulder of the road, was still as the engine thrummed. Her face, shrouded in the flickering darkness, was calm as the night air blew her hair into tangles. The opal necklace hung knotted from her fist as she reached for the windshield, reached for whatever wildness still lived inside her.

JOHN REINHART lives in the Weird, between now and never, collecting and protecting discarded treasures, and whistling combinations of every tune he knows. His poetry has recently been published in *Apeiron Review*, *The Vocabula Review*, *Black Heart Magazine*, *FishFood & LavaJuice Magazine*, *Star*Line*, and *Liquid Imagination*.

THE WORKS

Last night I wrote a symphony –
"Corrugated Recycles" I call it –
on the back of a pizza box.

It starts with strings playing pizzicato,
lumbers deep into horns covered in grease,
then cymbals, like giant pepperoni, crash.

The second movement creeps up the side
onto the top: "Cosmic Pizza" is all percussion,
rise and expansion, sustain, rest.

Movement three goes inward,
the most obscure and difficult part,
cluttered with crust and crumbs, real cheese,

stains too dark, too somber for any but celli,
summoning aged wood
like twelve year barreled bourbon.

Finally, up the inside lid, closure,
a simple melody to light the tunnel –
done in thirty minutes or it's free.

SPRING HOPES ETERNAL

The snow silences the melody so that if we listen
we can hear harmony in sleeping trees and icicles,
hibernating dreams and remembered promises...

Out of these depths, cracking the ice,
a seed introduces itself to sunlight,
shatters the surface of waiting, green with purpose,
and in this moment the fragile spiderweb of frost
melts, feeding the fledgling intention, infusing life
into tomorrow, into dreams, into hopes, into spring,
where blossoms blossom for immortal instants
and die into full, rich fruit of untainted light
shown through earth's prism, the promise of a promise.

NICK GAUDIO is a graduate of the University of Michigan's fiction program.

THUNDER

Dear Wife:

While you were gone, one night, I painted a naked woman.

That night, the night I painted a naked woman, the thunderstorms began.

Don't worry. It's all of little meaning to me now.

By "of little meaning," I suppose I should say "of little consequence," or containing little "that which gives most value to life." The thunderstorms were, yes, anomalous: stalwart, pregnant clouds that assaulted our little city for many hours. While within some clean-up crews I still find the occasional crazy who shrieks at me, "It wasn't just some circumstance! These were the hands of God!" I'm inclined to believe that attributing good and evil to a fairly long rain storm is pretty fucking stupid. You know this about me—moving on.

Perhaps it's because I'm not a zealot. Perhaps it's because I didn't lose a cat or a child or really anything of "substantial," or "quantifiable" value because of the floods. Perhaps it's because I no longer care enough for my own well-being to fear the unknown. But, just like everybody else, I like to think I see the world correctly; it's just that, in my world, "coincidence" is misleading, a cancer upon thought, and that there is nothing but "coincidence." To assign some weird duality to truth—between "weird" things that "happen" for a "reason" and how material events simply just fall into place—is vain and reckless and pitiable. It is false.

Accordingly, I want to stress that the symbolic weight of the woman to you, my wife—vulgarly: *what she means*—the importance of my heartbreak of your leaving is not quite appropriately shouldered by the image of some wanton, rapacious thunderhead rolling across the plains like the Tanks of the Gods, laying siege to our fair city for so many spins of the earth. These are "coincidences." Rather, if I were to say paint what this *means*—what you should *take* from this—I would smear my feces onto tissue paper, stick it to our ceiling and then go do something else.

Circumstance—no matter how beneficial it is to our daily worries—is not Meaning. And so, I ask myself, Why did you leave me? Why?

I'm sorry for bringing it up, because that's not my argument here. My argument, I'd say is that our desires for attaining wisdom, for laying it onto the web of the world, are complicated mechanisms to deal with our most complex fears. Or, in my case, non-fears. You're following.

I do miss the woman; I probably need these trivialities. I have no intention to impress sweetness upon you, because there is nothing sweet to behold. A sustained thunderstorm is not an earthquake. A thunderstorm is not John's Apocalypse; the woman could've easily stolen an umbrella and left me. Still. I'm absolutely positive that, in the re-telling of these events, I'm going to inadvertently gesture to some greater value in the storms—in their clouds' arrival, the exhaustive residence over the city, and their swift and immaculate departure. These nods are only beneficial because I probably made such flourishes at the time. When she touched me, I felt their necessity. I need to fully admit to you now that I am—bizarrely and incongruously—a man who both thinks too much and a boy who still romanticizes contact.

The girl, in apercu, wasn't holding an umbrella when she knocked on my door.

She wasn't prepared for the thunderstorm, in fact, at all. You must recall how storms often rolled in without any source or notice. How weathermen always predicated a twenty percent chance of rain and after five years of their insipid sweating on the television, I had vocally stopped watching altogether. I had a feeling, by the loose detachment in the way she stood, she too never really considered the weather. I opened the door.

Her shoes were gratuitously burnished, silver. Her legs, long and smooth, without blemish. Her hair was highly manicured, hung suggestively like a curtain of onyx, over the left third of her face. (Here I am again, gesturing). Her eyes a deep and unyielding green. Under the white gauze of her summer dress—what would have turned translucent if she broke into even a glistening—she was without a bra. Her nipples, visible, were dime-sized, equally petite. Her beauty, in such magnitude, suggested uselessness—impracticality—to me. How could she wake, how could she walk, or eat, or perform all the bodily grotesques in this cold and stinking world? I was uncertain—especially considering, you know, how I generally prefer blondes.

There stood a beacon, an angel of all good things, and I was very lonely, having eaten a cold American cheese sandwich for dinner, alone, in that old terrycloth robe. I stood in the foyer for a moment, gawking stupidly at her.

"I have a favor to ask you," she said. Her voice had the cool brevity of a doorbell.

I said yes—or I believe I said yes—and then, "You're not selling Bibles?"

"No," she introduced herself with a handshake. "I'd like you to paint me."

Perhaps, if I could paint anything at all successfully, even today, I would recreate what I remember at this moment: behind her face, the first puffy wall of a cold front moving in from the west. A harbinger. A puff-ball. The cloud, one large island, silently pulling closer. In the light of sunset, its edges had softened into a glowing, sublimated gold. I would really work on that cloud.

No, I would paint her face above, the face of an idol. Huffy intellectuals would say, "She represents the virgin." And that would be the gesture I would be making, she was perfect and clean in the way the Bible suggests Mary was perfect. I cannot think of her as my savior, my mother, or simply a woman who arrived one day and needed badly for a novice to paint her nude body.

I had never considered this before—painting—and I admit, I was clever enough to say, "You want me to paint you right here?" as though such artistry was something I was familiar with, and for my genius to thrive specific conditions needed to be met. What those were I dare not consider now. I'm just thankful that they hadn't existed before. Knowing me, there would be too many stupid qualifications and our romance would've shriveled. Silly.

Let me explain why I mishandled the truth, my dear wife. The angel, the evening, the sunset. Then the dull, bachelor stink of my apartment, my crawling skin, my matted, shaggy, fifteen-year-old terrycloth robe from a JC Penny catalog. The schism between beauty and not-beauty seemed to be manifest at the doorway. Lying is okay, if it's the only method of escape.

I was standing there, at the mouth of a wormhole into Earth dimension three-thousand-two. I was looking in, where all things are insane, illogical and therefore malicious and beautiful. She, the girl, politely cleared her throat. Any idiot could slop a cursory replication of this moment on a canvas and somebody would call it art. I don't mean to be critical here, only that I sometimes still think only minimal talent is necessary when recreating reality. Also, I was naked under the robe.

The girl noticed the vector my brain had taken me, "I want you to paint me, nude, inside your home," she grabbed my arm. "Do you understand? Am I being clear?"

I didn't ask "Why?"

Though I suppose now it would have been irrelevant, and possibly very stupid to question a near naked woman at my door. Still, I hesitated. (I consider art, essentially, an act of human connection, always predicated on a vast, common fear of death. The cortege of art follows one, common sentiment, and what is sentiment but an appeal to appreciate this antiseptic flicker in the universe—no matter how commonplace the Hallmark Card might be, it is a gift between two beings that shakes both, albeit lightly, at the shoulders. And if you didn't know this, it's simply because you didn't ask.)

"Hey," she said. "Hey? Are you with me?"

"I'm not a painter," I admitted. "You must be confusing me with somebody else."

"All the more reason to paint," she said, turning back to me, walking up, her nose inches from my own. I was silent.

The girl stood looking at me. She knew that she had bested me. A cold draft would have been appropriate—to punctuate the moment—but none such relief came. "Well?" she asked.

"Come in," I finally said. "And I'll try to paint you."

As we walked farther inside a place that once was yours and mine, I tossed my dirty clothes into a pile in the corner of the television room. The television sat flickering. We sat awkwardly on the couch. After perhaps three minutes, I said, "I don't have any materials...to paint you."

And sure enough, in her giant purse—have I neglected to mention the enormous satchel?—she pulled a single, unwrinkled sheet of standard white paper, a thin paintbrush and a dark gray tube of acrylic paint titled "Shade of black." She sat the materials on the floor, noting my coffee table was too cluttered with bachelor-themed magazines, generic soda cans, half of an old American cheese sandwich. She sat properly, surveying the table, my privacy laid bare; her legs crossed at the knee, a single foot bobbing.

She said, "I've anticipated that. I brought some."

"Is this the only color I'll need?" I asked. I pulled my robe closed at the neck.

"It's the only color *I* need," she said. "It's the only color I want. To capture me."

Capture? Could I *capture*? This girl had mistaken my identity for some other person, some other man, who must have been a painter with my name. Some juvenile, spasmodic philosopher at the college, quite scrawny, held himself like a sultan and spoke deeply, but dully. Had you met him? Your name crossed my mind.

"Alright," I told the girl.

I was happy to take advantage of the mix-up of identity, but only in regard to what might become anonymously sexual. There are still scars all over my past. I had still been posturing (or maybe, still knew enough to know to maintain posture). I told the girl I couldn't rightfully create the art without two caveats being addressed.

"One," I said, "I feel like I need to know you better."

This wasn't meant to be innuendo, though I'm sure now she considered it so. She pursed her lips, a moue, "That can be done."

"And two," I said, "I am probably not person you think I am."

"I know who you are," she said.

We left it at that.

"Then you can understand the dilemma," I eventually said. "This is a moral problem. And I was fired. Do you know why?"

"Your wife. She was cheating on you."

I shuddered deeply thinking of it, of our trials. "It was more than that," I said, and I believe now more so than ever that I had been defending you.

The girl looked around the room and rubbed the small soft chasm between her neck and shoulders, "How about the abbreviated version."

"There is no abbreviated version," I said.

"Give it a try."

I hadn't been proud of what I'd done until this moment, when my virility was questioned. "I struck the man she had...you know," I said.

"And what exactly, had he done, after?" she asked, a

wash of excitement lifting her eyes.

"He stole my wife." You.

She moved closer to me on the couch and put her hand on my thigh, "Tell me more."

"It's not important now," I said. "Only that he was careless and aggressive and I wasn't in the mood for that sort of behavior that day. It was a very nice day and he had ruined it by telling me how fateful it was that she and he got together."

"Sexy," the girl said. The consonants hung between us. Outside, perhaps the first flash of lightning.

The room snapped blue, a color that suggested a sound that inevitably went unheard, the trumpeter of thunder too far in the distance; whoever, wherever he was, he stood behind a thick plate of glass. The room eventually turned dark, and our silence reawakened, the tension in the room filled it with soft, artificial heat. The last pink beams of sunlight were then swallowed up by the clouds and the night.

"I brought some candles," the girl said.

She had already lit the flambeau by the time I stumbled out the words, "That's pretty Victorian."

"Yes, you're right," she said. She lifted the white dress by its thin straps, before I was able to utter any cogent response. She reclined into the armrest of the couch and brought a finger to her red lips as my jaw relaxed, outside the rain began to unload in torrents. I stood and moved a folding chair across the room. She laid down on my orange suede couch, a fireball in herself; she had been completely nude under the dress. I coughed and grabbed a magazine to work as my easel. "It's really coming down out there," she said. Reveling a little in my awkward, the girl winked again. Diablerie.

I began with a swipe that marked the stream-lined silhouette between her ankle and hip. The brush dipped in paint again and her legs were formed. Thunder began murmuring outside, and the sounds of rain against the roof hushed and pelted in dynamic waves. She lit a cigarette without asking, watched me with a fairly playful skepticism: she had kept the silver heels on to the same effect.

"This may be better than I originally thought," I said, painting now the outlines of her breasts, never having been so talented at drawing anything so round in my life.

"I'd just like it to be honest," she said. "Just be honest or you'll fail completely."

And, in this way, I tried my best to show her how much I appreciated her unexpected arrival in my life. My room, since you had left, had felt like some passage from one thing to the next to the next, then to my own death, began to feel less like a catacomb and more like a trail through a wet and leafy forest. I withdrew myself deeply from the scene, allowed my hands to present on paper the form I saw.

"Am I doing this to your liking?" I asked, focused still, "Will you tell me?"

"No," she said. "It'll ruin the mood."

And until I finished the painting, the only sounds in the living room were the gushes and howls provided by the apocalyptic rain. I couldn't help but think of the clouds over our city not as sinister, the rumbles of thunder as prophetic agents for some higher being that was not all love, but all confusion, all naivety in that way somehow approaching a variable called tenderness.

I flipped the single white sheet of paper and handed it to the girl. The result of my efforts a post-modernist approach without my realizing as much. All outlines, no shading.

Her face on the paper consisted of four lines, two for her green eyes; one arched and inaccurate slit as her nose and a wide and buckled down thing for her mouth. The white paper had the quality of her skin already. There was very little shading I felt needed to capture her. I had really wanted the color red, for her lips, for the plate of blushing skin that spanned from her collarbone down in a sort of triangle between her breasts. I had wanted silver to color those heels. I was at least, thankful for my memory: I'd always remember this.

"This is exactly what I wanted," she said, remaining on her side on my couch.

"I'm glad to have been honest," I said.

"Well, you could have been a little more expressive here, with my face."

A crack of thunder shook the room, lightning that felt as close as the driveway.

We looked at each other. We had both expected, probably, that over this last hour or so, the heavy rain would relax.

"I need a frame for it," the girl said.

I opened a drawer in a stand beside the couch. A picture of you and I smiling in our old suburban yard—the sunlight behind the camera-person causing us to squint. The neighborhood a dull and flat thing in the distance. I removed the picture and handed her the frame.

"This will do," she said.

I wadded up the picture of you, tossing it in the corner, with all my dirty clothes.

When we made love that night on the couch, her body yielding to me as easily as the brush had upon the paper, I had been a calm, unexpectedly tender lover. There are now, inevitably, more colors than Shade of Black that I need to describe everything else. The candles burned, little torches, licked the walls with a heavy orange. Her eyes a spring green. Her touch, I would paint too, a color I can only describe as polychrome, a color I decided much later felt like sparks and may someday, when I choose to paint the scene require the melting of some sort of precious metal. Of course, I'm being cheeky.

When we finished, we lay silently with each other, the thunder and rain had not yet become tiresome, had not ceased in growing in their intensity. "This storm?" she asked me.

"In the morning it'll be gone."

"So at dawn," she agreed, already an apparition. "We'll never see each other again."

The girl was inevitably right. The storm was like a promise one intends to keep for one night.

The rain continued to plunge and we fell asleep, holding these vows as close as our bodies, for reasons that seem now more than human. You see, it seems to me that our natures are moral-seeking, and for that we seek meaning. We testify in our routines that we will never connect, will only celebrate our loneliness with art and touch, will never return to each other upon waking from our little, unimportant dreams. But waking, as I did, with a crack of thunder so near the window, with my walls trembling, my arms without the warmth of her body: I woke to find myself alone again, a paintbrush dipped in some inky residue stuck to the cover of an old Hustler in some damned, foul-smelling apartment. And the rain; it kept going. It kept raining outside and I invariably considered you once more.

RYAN FAVATA is a recent graduate of Rollins College, where he majored in English and minored in Creative Writing. He was the 2013 recipient of the Laura van den Berg Scholarship and winner of the 2014 Arden Goettling/ Academy of American Poets Prize. His work has also appeared in *One Throne Magazine*, *Synchronized Chaos*, and *Ricochet Magazine*. He currently resides in Winter Park, Florida.

AMERICANS ABROAD

I breathe in the 1st century-ness of the Piazza Navona
tired, and take a sip of wine. I glance over my shoulder at
a small group of Romans smoking by a fountain—

Fontana—and take note of how
they smoke, looking down at my own cigarette.
One girl leans into the group, saying something

they erupt in laughter. They leave.
There are many cigarettes I've cherished, without
a doubt, and this could be one of them.

Three weeks from now I'll tell my friends
it was indeed the best smoke I've ever had.
No no—first I'll ask where they've been, if their stories

are well-travelled; then, and only then, will I decide
if the Romans sat down with me, drinking for hours,
telling me there is where earth and heaven met.

THE UNFORGIVEN

Today I decided to write
at a local coffee shop adjacent
to a bar I frequent. I've never
been one for writing in public, coffee

shops in particular, but my house
feels stale today and smells of the
pasta and meatballs I cooked last
night while watching some

documentary on the migratory
habits of seagulls. I've eyed this
coffee shop many times, with its
hipsters cradling lattes and

chiseling at their keyboards with
eyes that could only be saying
whatever they are writing is
more profound, deep, spiritual,

groovy, and substantial, if not
merely longer than anything
I could or ever will write. But that's
fine. To be honest, I've grown tired

of the hipster bashing. The guys are quiet,
unless in their circles, and the girls
look like Aubrey Hepdurn, in fact
The one across from me could be

her reincarnated. *Audrey Hepburn.*
I look around in shame, hoping no
one saw my unforgivable typo, or
especially the woman herself in

front of me, with her short shining
brunette strands, staring off into space.I look at her and
plead for forgiveness
in my head—promising to watch

Breakfast at Timothy's ten,
maybe twenty, times in penance.